Flowing Water,
Uncommon Birth

Christian Baptism in a Post-Christian Culture

Samuel Torvend

AUGSBURG FORTRESS

FLOWING WATER, UNCOMMON BIRTH
Christian Baptism in a Post-Christian Culture

Editor: Suzanne Burke
Cover design: Laurie Ingram
Interior design: Laurie Ingram / Timothy W. Larson
Cover photo: Flowing River Water Over Rocks © istockphoto.com / BanksPhotos

ISBN 978–0–8066–7063–8

Manufactured in the U.S.A.

17   16   15   14   13   12   11   1   2   3   4   5   6   7

For E. Silas and Alice Kjesbu Torvend,
father and mother who brought me to holy baptism,

for Rex Torvend Rainsberger,
nephew and godson whose light shines brightly,

for Sean Alair Horner,
partner in Christian faith and life,

In memory of S. Anita Stauffer,
colleague in baptismal archeology—
dead to this world yet alive to God.
(1948–2007)

Contents

Introduction:
Why Baptize?

Here the innocent sheep,
cleansed by the heavenly water,
are marked by the hand of the Good Shepherd.

On January 5, 2003, the festival of the Epiphany, Rex Torvend
Rainsberger was baptized in Seattle, Washington, on a cool but sunny
day. Surrounded by the worshiping assembly, relatives, family friends,
and his parents, the two-month-old infant was carried by his mother
to a font of water where a large beeswax candle stood burning next
to it. In his white garment, he was handed to his Filipina-American
godmother. The presider exhorted the parents to bring their son to
worship, to teach him the Ten Commandments, the Creed, and the
Lord's Prayer, to place in his hands the Bible, and to provide for his
instruction in the Christian faith in communion with the church.

The presider then offered thanks over the local water in the font,
water that comes from the Cedar River flowing out of the Cascade
Mountains. The whole assembly renounced "all the forces of evil" and
then confessed an ancient Roman baptismal creed. His Norwegian-
American grandfather poured water over his head as he was baptized
"in the name of the Father, and of the Son, and of the Holy Spirit."

Large hands were laid on his tiny brow as the minister offered thanks to God for his new life and prayed for the outpouring of the Spirit upon him. A cross, the first century emblem of a humiliating death first devised in the ancient Persian Empire, was traced over his forehead. A small candle, lit from the large one, was given to his father. A prayer was offered for his parents, and then a member of the assembly declared that Rex, the infant, had been made a "priest" so that he might "bear God's creative and redeeming Word to the world." He yawned, long and deeply, as the assembly announced that they had received him as "a worker in the kingdom of God." Then, quoting the words of the risen Christ, the presider said, "Peace be with you," and the whole congregation erupted into loud chatter, shaking hands, kissing, embracing, laughing, blotting out a few tears, cooing over the baby—a small, contained, and controlled chaos.

Throughout this ancient ritual, Rex did not cry out once. He simply gurgled once in a while. He appeared docile if not oblivious to the questions, the washing, the hand-laying, the cross traced on his head, the burning lights surrounding him, the declaration made over his small body. So much ritual action. So many prayers and expectations for a newborn child. A light-bearer? A priest? A worker in the reign of God? Honestly, did anyone really think about what they were saying when all these things were affirmed on behalf of the yawning infant? Or is it possible that few of us were really paying attention to the words and actions and were focused rather on the charm of the newborn? Or were we wondering if his eighty-two-year-old grandfather would begin weeping as he poured water on the head of his only grandchild—so incredibly tender and so precious the moment across the generations? Or is it possible that all the words and actions—the intense focus for one full day on this little boy's life—were simply superfluous in light of the bottom line: *he was safe now*—safe with God for all eternity. Whether he died in eight minutes or eighty-five years, he would not be lost to God or his parents or the church but would, in the consoling words of the Reformation hymn, "stand among the glorious heavenly band of every tribe and nation" (*Evangelical Lutheran Worship* #442; *Hymnal 1982* #298).

Here, then, we ask the questions of the catechism: *What does this mean?* My godson's English, Danish, Norwegian, and Swiss ancestors lived in cultures that understood themselves in some way to be Christian. They believed that baptism was a normative action through which a person was not only identified religiously but also ethnically. Thus, Swiss Calvinists, English Anglicans, and Scandinavian Lutherans have practiced the baptism of infants for close to five hundred years. Indeed, they did not depart from the practice of Eastern Orthodoxy and Roman Catholicism. Yet the European churches of the magisterial reformation are now almost empty, Christianity perceived as a cultural artifact of Europe's rich heritage or as the willing consort of colonial oppression throughout the globe. Indeed, if there is any lively growth on the landscape of European religions, it is among Muslims and Christian Pentecostals. One must look to Africa, India, Asia, and Latin America—the southern hemisphere—to find a flourishing and diverse Christianity.

In North America, a few regions seem to be saturated with or at least hospitable toward religion. Yet church and cultural historians suggest that the pervasive presence of the film and television industry and the Internet have initiated succeeding generations, since 1945, into a cultural ethos—a way of experiencing, thinking about, and living life—that may have little if any relationship to the gospel of Jesus Christ. *What does this mean?* What does it mean to practice Christian baptism at a time in which one's identity and purpose in life are being "constructed" or shaped, from the moment of one's birth, by a constant stream of visual, musical, and textual messages created by those who want one thing and one thing only: a profit? Is the way in which our ancestors thought about the relationship between religion and national identity no longer helpful? Is there a way in which the claims of Christian baptism are eroded by or assimilated into a larger and more powerful cultural ethos? Has it become increasingly difficult to discern anything distinctive within the Christian baptismal community—in its way of understanding life and living with others—that would distinguish it from the values or practices portrayed daily on television? Should he choose to do so, my godson could watch "reality" shows every day; programs whose one clear purpose is to demonstrate the ways in which human beings can eliminate or fight with each other, shows which sanction the diminishment of shared life and the common good. Of course, such programs make perfect sense in a cultural context where the strong survive and those alleged to be weak perish. *What does this mean?*

Some of my colleagues in the academy claim that Christianity has had its day. At best, it is perceived as an interesting historical artifact or a coping mechanism for weak-minded people who need strength in numbers. Indeed, it can be difficult for some people—inside and outside the academy—to imagine that curious, intelligent, and world-engaged human beings can find any life-giving meaning or purpose within a Christian community. Here's the sad thing: there is a good measure of truth in what they claim. Christian communities and their leaders can offer mind-numbing and soul-destroying experiences of legalism, neurotic leadership, over-weaning optimism, dreadful pessimism, exclusion, censorship, ugly music, terrible art, techno-pop, uninspired preaching, and plain inattentiveness to real human need. They can reject the use of reason in the search for truth and dismiss what they perceive as any threatening claim made by scientists, historians, and artists. Good heavens! Who would want to be baptized into that way of life?

Yet what of those young people who, with increasing numbers, sit in the back pews of the church where I serve? What of the psychologist, teacher, banker, bike messenger, webmaster, poet, school bus driver, and single mother—all remarkably thoughtful people, all horrified by the mind-numbing and soul-destroying capacities of Christianity—who are nonetheless curious about the Christian way of life? What does it mean, in this increasingly secularized culture, where religion is pushed out of the public square, that they watch what goes on in our parish week after week? And then, in an off-hand remark, one of them says, "I have some questions for you. Do you have time for a chat?" How, then, does one think about formation in faith within a culture where religion is considered "a coping mechanism for weak-minded people who need strength in numbers"? How does one begin to listen to their questions and concerns when Christians, throughout much of their history, have simply imagined that they were doing people a favor by baptizing them? How does one listen carefully, with the distinct possibility in mind, that there might not be a ready answer to the question posed? How does one learn *to listen* when pastors, priests, ministers, preachers, and teachers have been trained to speak rather than be silent; when they have been trained with the notion that they have most if not all the answers? *What does this mean?*

In the years after my godson's baptism, I have been thinking about that act and his life. Will he ever be invited to reflect on the deep meanings of those words and actions which surrounded him in his second month of life? Will he encounter teachers or pastors or companions who are what the ancient church called "mystagogues"—people practiced in the art of revealing the meaning of ritual for life in the world? Perhaps he is already being disposed toward this encounter when his parents help him conserve water and explore, with care, the natural world in which he lives. Perhaps in the many lessons of daily etiquette, he is learning how to respect the dignity of others and respond to their needs. Perhaps, now, as a parochial school student, he is growing into his Christian identity as he learns that Jesus loves "all the children of the world," not just his circle of friends. Perhaps, as he opens his hands at the altar to receive the Good Shepherd's food and drink, he is learning to share his own food and drink with those who have little, with "the least of these."

With my nephew and his parents and grandparents, I live in a region of the continent where Christians are a minority of the general population, and where those who celebrate the ancient rituals and seasons of the church are even smaller. And so I wonder: how is our baptismal preparation, the celebration of baptism, and ongoing baptismal and eucharistic formation shaping a people who will not only survive but flourish—perhaps in small ways—in a culture which remains skeptical of religion, religious people, and religious communities. For a moment I find some consolation in the fact the movement which was first called "The Way" and then "Christian" began among an incredibly small group of people who had so little and yet so much: some fresh local water, a collection of stories and sayings, a bit of baked bread, a cup of wine, and two or three or maybe more gathered in the presence of the shepherd and guardian of their souls.

These reflections on Christian baptism draw on the work of biblical and liturgical scholars, church historians, sociologists of religion, theologians, poets, cultural analysts, film-makers, and writers, the witness of the New Testament, the sermons, hymns, and architecture of early Christians, ancient and modern liturgical texts, medieval mystics, reformation leaders, and modern martyrs and reformers. In the outline of this little book, one may glimpse the early Christian pattern of baptismal preparation, baptismal and eucharistic celebration, and ongoing formation for life in the world—what was called then and more recently the catechumenal process, the practice of intentional formation leading to baptism and flowing from it.

The reformation of the sixteenth century began with questions—with troubling enquiries which called into question the received practices and wisdom of the previous five hundred years. It should come as no surprise to us that the reformers, so keenly versed in the imaginative world of the Bible, would create change with a few questions. Indeed, one might claim that the origins of Christianity itself can be traced to a question and a practice. In response to Peter's preaching on the day of Pentecost, the gathered assembly asked, "What should we do?" And Peter said to them, "Repent and be baptized every one of you in the name of Jesus Christ … for the promise is for you, for your children, and for all who are far away" (Acts 2:37-39).

Be welcome, then, to these reflections on that one-time event which, nonetheless, welcomes the baptized into a lifetime engagement with its many riches.

1

The Baptism of Jesus in River and Cross

Here springs the fountain of life
In which the entire world is washed—
From Christ's wounds it takes its origin and source.

Using water to welcome people into a community was not invented by Christians. Evidence from the first century indicates that Jews washed converts to Judaism and leaders of the mystery religions bathed people as a form of initiation. The gospels present us with the figure of John the Baptizer who washed Palestinian Jews in the waters of the Jordan River—not as a form of initiation into Judaism, but as a means of marking people who looked with hope for the coming of God in the midst of much economic, social, and political disarray. After all, the Roman Empire had occupied the land given by God to the chosen people for some sixty-five years before the birth of Jesus of Nazareth. Conquered by the Roman general Pompey, Palestine became a client kingdom of the empire: occupied by the Roman army, indebted with imperial taxes, awash in the many gods of the Greeks and Romans, impoverished and humiliated. While the Romans allowed a measure of religious freedom, any religious community which proclaimed that their god held their ultimate loyalty was in for trouble. To worship one god—the God of Abraham and Sarah, Moses and Miriam—was to question if not deny the ultimate power of the Roman emperor, a human who referred to himself as "Son of God," "Lord of lords," and "Savior of the world." In that world then, how could one worship—give one's body, mind, and spirit—to the kingdom of the emperor *and* the kingdom of God? How could one live with a divided heart? For in the imperial kingdom there was only one lord and savior: Caesar, a man who imposed "peace" through military violence.

In this highly-charged context, the evangelists narrate the baptism of Jesus in the Jordan (Mark 1:9-11; Matt. 3:13-17; Luke 3:21-22; John 1:29-34). That river, so small when one actually sees it, was filled with profound meaning for the Jews of Palestine. It was there that the people annually commemorated their ancient passing through the Red Sea, from servile oppression under another imperial ruler into the freedom which God made possible, into their formation as one people under God, their shepherd, their ruler. John practiced a baptism in the Jordan, a river filled with the meaning of the Exodus, as a crying out to God for a new deliverance, for a new passage in a time marked by chaos and despair. In Mark, the earliest gospel written, the evangelist narrates the first public appearance of Jesus:

> In those days Jesus came from Nazareth of Galilee and was baptized by John in the Jordan. And just as he was coming up out of the water, he saw the heavens torn apart and the Spirit descending like a dove on him. And a voice came from heaven, "You are my Son, the Beloved; with you I am well pleased."
>
> And the Spirit immediately drove him out into the wilderness . . .
>
> Now after John was arrested, Jesus came to Galilee, proclaiming the good news of God, and saying, "The time is ful-

filled, and the kingdom of God has come near; repent, and believe in the good news."

As Jesus passed along the Sea of Galilee, he saw Simon and his brother Andrew casting a net into the sea—for they were fishermen. And Jesus said to them, "Follow me and I will make you fish for people." And immediately they left their nets and followed him. (Mark 1:9-18)

A water-washed public servant

While the story of Jesus' baptism is relatively short, it reveals a significant measure of surprising meanings. Jesus comes to John and is baptized by him. He does not baptize himself as if such a washing were simply a human activity announcing one's status or personal commitments. Jesus enters the Jordan waters, filled with the memory of slavery and liberation, suffering and surprising release, food and drink in the desert, an eternal covenant, and the promise of a land flowing with God's own milk and honey. He is washed in the great hope for God's coming to a people who "dwell in darkness and the shadow of death." He stands in solidarity with his Jewish brothers and sisters who followed John down to the water's edge, all turned, as it were, toward the coming of God to God's suffering people. With Roman cultural values and military control pouring in like many troubling waters, this baptism could be recognized as a singular calling out for God's powerful presence: "Give ear, O Shepherd of Israel, you who lead Joseph like a flock! . . .Stir up your might, and come to save us! Restore us, O God; let your face shine, that we may be saved" (Ps. 80:1-3). As there had been redemption in ancient Egypt—so this Jordan washing seemed to proclaim—let there be deliverance in this present age.

Perhaps Mark's account could have ended there: Jesus was baptized by John. And yet, notes the evangelist, there was more: the Spirit fell upon Jesus as the Spirit fell upon Israel's priests, prophets, and rulers, empowering Jesus, anointing him—that is, marking him—in public for a public purpose. Jesus was not baptized into a private, "spiritual" relationship with God, a relationship separate from Israel's history, scripture, rituals, and community. Rather, he was baptized with others and publicly declared by an unnamed voice from heaven as the Son, the Beloved, a reference to the servant of the Lord in Isaiah: "Here is my servant, whom I uphold, my chosen, in whom my soul delights; I have put my spirit upon him; he will bring forth justice to the nations" (42:1). Not unlike the ancient prophet Elijah, Jesus too enters into the wilderness for forty days—a number significant in the Hebrew Scriptures: forty days in which a new creation emerged from the destructive flood (Gen. 6–8); Moses' sojourn of forty days with God on the mountain (Exod. 24); the Hebrew wandering in the wilderness for forty years (Num. 14). In the desert, Jesus experiences what other prophets of God underwent: a forty-day period of testing. Note the movement of the narrative. From his washing in Jordan's water, he enters into the formative experience of the wilderness. From the wilderness experience, he enters into public life with this message: "The time is fulfilled, and the kingdom of God has come near; repent, and believe in the good news" (Mark 1:15). *Jesus is baptized, marked by Spirit and voice, for public life.* There is no getting around the trajectory of the narrative. This washing in the river Jordan did not initiate him into a private relationship with God, a human soul communing with divine being. Indeed, Jesus had no need to "accept God as his personal Lord and Savior." Rather, from the waters of the Jordan he entered into public life with this purpose: the proclamation and enactment of the nearness of God's reign. This may have been "bad" news for those who worshiped the reign of Caesar but, notes Mark, it was "good news" for those who longed to experience God's merciful and life-giving presence, a gospel so different than the message proclaimed by the Roman emperor who thought he was a god worthy of worship.

Blessed be God's kingdom

In many Christian homes and churches, there can be much talk of *love* as the central message of Jesus and the abiding mark of contemporary Christians. Most biblical scholars would say otherwise—and for good reason. Mark, Matthew, and Luke are of one voice when they note that Jesus' public life, initiated in baptism, focused on the coming reign of God (Mark 1:14-15; Matt. 4:12-17; Luke 4:14-15). This is not to say that Jesus never mentioned love or peace or forgiveness. Indeed, these were and remain powerful symbols alive in the Christian imagination. It is to say, however, that Jesus proclaimed in word and action the nearness of God's rule: "Jesus came to Galilee, proclaiming the good news of God, and saying, 'The time is fulfilled, and the kingdom of God has come near; repent, and believe in the good news'" (Mark 1:14-15). The Episcopal *Book of Common Prayer* highlights the centrality of this proclamation at the very beginning of the liturgy. The presider sings, "Blessed be God: Father, Son, and Holy Spirit," to which the assembly responds with one voice, "And blessed be God's kingdom, now and forever. Amen." But *what does this mean?* What did Jesus mean when he proclaimed the advent of God's reign? What does it mean to sing of God's kingdom at the beginning of the Eucharist?

One simple but complex answer to the question is this: Jesus' use of the term "kingdom" or "reign" implies a social and a political reality. Kings and queens rule kingdoms; they rule a group of people. At the same time, Jesus' use of the term "God" implies a theological reality: a living, active power and presence within yet beyond this world, within and yet beyond the many words we use to understand and live within this mystery. It is *God's kingdom or reign*, not my kingdom or your kingdom; not the emperor's reign or the general's rule. And this: God's reign or rule *encompasses the whole of life*, not just one compartment of life. It is a presence personal and communal, one that seeps into and shapes the economic, social, and political dimensions of life. That is, where God is ruling, where God is present, all of life—*all of life*—is shaped and ordered by that presence.

That can be a claim hard for modern North American Christians to swallow. Too many times we imagine that faith or Christianity or religion is one significant dimension of life, but one that is separate from, for instance, our economic or sexual or political sensibilities. Not so in the world in which Jesus lived. In Jesus' time and culture as a Jew, all life is one and lived out in the presence of God. The human being could not be divided into the neat compartments of body versus soul versus mind. The God who brought all things into being was attentive to all, not just one dimension of life (e.g., the inanimate soul)—the entire person who lived and lives within economic, political, and social dynamics of a particular culture. Thus Jesus teaches his followers to pray, "Give us this day our daily bread" (a physical necessity shaped by economic realities). He gathers a diverse array of persons as his companions (a social reality incorporating different political views: Simon the Zealot, a Rome hater, and Matthew, a Rome collaborator). He offers free healing to the poor, the very people who could never afford the ancient healer's fee (a physical, social, and economic reality). Indeed, when Jesus proclaims the nearness of God's reign, he is not pointing to a physical place (such as the Kingdom of Great Britain as found on a map) but to the active presence, benevolent and merciful, of God in, with, and through all of life. Consequently, when the newly-baptized Jesus announces the coming of God's rule, he is pointing to this significant meaning: *God is coming toward, advancing toward humans* who yearn for, who cry out for wholeness, health, integrity. Such words—wholeness and health—expand the meaning of that ancient and powerful symbol, salvation.

Everyone is searching for you

One could argue that if Jesus' central proclamation was the advance of God's life-giving reign in the midst of much anxiety, impoverishment, and diminishment, then the rest of the gospel story demonstrates the manner in which God's presence was revealed to Jesus' contemporaries: through Jesus' words and actions. From the waters of the Jordan, Jesus emerges as a public servant of the reign of God. Yet for the evangelists, writing from the perspective of his resurrection, Jesus not only pointed to but also embodied that reign in the manner of his life. The message he proclaimed saturated his life so completely that in experiencing him, one encountered and continues to encounter the very mystery of God and God's presence.

Along with the other gospel writers, Mark demonstrates the manner in which Jesus, water-washed and marked for public life, embodied God's presence. First, he is not a loner, a maverick. He calls ordinary people to join him as companions: "Follow me," he says to Simon and Andrew, James and John, "and I will make you fish for people" (1:17). While Mark narrates opposition to Jesus, he also clearly demonstrates that women and men were drawn to him, "For he taught them as one having authority, and not as the scribes" (1:22). That Jesus called and calls a community of followers into existence serves as a potent critique of the notion that Christian identity can be reduced to "Jesus and me," an individual relationship between the solitary soul and the solitary Savior. In the reign of God, we are together since we have been created by God as social beings, mutually dependent for life, health, and well-being. Jesus calls a diverse group of people together as his companions in his public service to the reign of the God of Israel.

Second, Jesus speaks of this reign in parables and sayings. He does not offer strategies, statements, or business models for the effective marketing of his message. His language is poetic rather than prosaic, more evocative than explanatory. The reign of God—since it comes from God and at God's initiative—does not necessarily confirm or support the conventional wisdom of the local culture, be it Palestinian, Roman, or American. When Jesus speaks of God's rule in human life, he startles the listener with unconventional images of God's presence. Accepted assumptions of God's relationship with humankind and the relationships between persons of different gender, race, economic status, and religious observance are reversed. For example, no observant Jew would expect or even want to receive hospitality and assistance from a Samaritan, a person considered "unclean," and from an ethnically and religiously "inferior" community. Yet Jesus seems to suggest in his parable that God opposes such "conventional" thinking and the discriminatory practices which issued from such thinking. In the reign of God, his parable affirms, there are no "clean" and "unclean," no worthy and unworthy, no insider and outsider. In the rule of God, there is only benevolence and compassion for the many rather than the few. In the kingdom of God, there is no culturally or religiously constructed division between "some-bodies" and "no-bodies." There is to be one people, guided by their one shepherd, who offers a merciful way into the future.

Third, Jesus is drawn to those who were regularly overlooked, forgotten, or feared in his world. He exorcises those possessed with unclean and tormenting spirits, heals the sick, cleanses lepers, restores paralyzed limbs, shares meals with despised tax collectors, defends his hungry followers who pluck grain on the sabbath, feeds impoverished peasants with bread and fish, and works on the day of rest by curing a man's withered hand. While some voices in the Christian tradition have claimed that Jesus' actions are demonstrations of his divinity, other voices suggest that his free healing, his open meal practice, and his alliance with those considered marginal and "unclean" members of his society were palpable and thus powerful demonstrations of the nearness of God's rule and presence in human life. Those shunned because of chronic physical or mental illness are restored to community; those who would die without nourishment are raised to life with his feeding; those who seek the knowledge of God are enlightened; those who bear terrible shame and guilt are released through Jesus' word of forgiveness; those considered "second-class citizens" in the kingdom of Caesar—women, children, the poor, the chronically sick, the elderly—discover, to their utter surprise, that they are the beloved children of God endowed with an eternal dignity. To say the least, those who welcomed Jesus' words and actions responded with thanksgiving, "spread the word" (Mark 1:45), and praised God (Mark 2:12).

And yet, and yet—Jesus met with misunderstanding and opposition. While the history of Christianity is marked by Christians declaring that people other than themselves opposed Jesus (e.g., Jews and pagan Romans), a closer look at the text reveals something else. Mark notes that Jesus' own family and his disciples misunderstood, questioned, or rejected his mission. Those who seemed to be closest to him may have received his message and witnessed his life yet could not fully understand and support the implications of his public work. With a history of anti-Judaism alive among Christians, the opposition of Jewish scribes (interpreters of the Mosaic Law) and Jewish Pharisees has been commonplace. Mark notes that the scribes charge Jesus with blasphemy when he forgives sins (2:1-12) and the Pharisees criticize him when he allows his companions to pluck grain on the sabbath (2:23-28). When they watch him cure someone on the sabbath, they "conspire to destroy him" (3:1-6). Townspeople become fearful and ask him to leave their neighborhood (5:14-20) and even the people with whom he grew up in Nazareth reject him (6:1-6). Members of his family seek to restrain him, for people were saying, "He has gone out of his mind" (3:21). Even the disciples he called to join in his public mission are uncomprehending to the point where he asks them: "Do you not yet understand?" (8:21). While Peter boldly claims that "You are the Messiah" (8:29), he will, nonetheless, abandon Jesus and deny his association with him. Indeed, when Jesus announces to his disciples three times that he will suffer for his proclamation of the reign of God (8:31—9:1; 9:30-32; 10:32-34), their response is to reject his announcement and jockey for positions of power (9:33-37; 10:35-45). Even those closest to him fail to perceive that his embodiment of the reign of God will lead to his death at the hands of the Roman imperial army.

A public witness silenced, so it seemed

All this is to say that while some receive him with gratitude, others—even his closest followers—fail to grasp that there will be conflict and that the baptism which inaugurated his public ministry will be sealed with his baptism in the cross: "Are you able to drink the cup that I drink, or be baptized with the baptism that I am baptized with?" (Mark 10:38). That is, did they fail to recognize the trajectory of his public life? Did they fail to grasp that the one who proclaimed God's presence with the "unclean," with sinners, with all those who had been led to believe that they were no-bodies in the kingdom of Caesar would himself be put to death in the most "unclean" and humiliating manner possible: in a public execution, among the dying and the dead, outside of the city—that place of desolation, abandoned by the ancient gods? Did they fail to grasp the tension between two kingdoms, two "cultures"—one in which power is used to dominate and control for personal or national gain and the other in which power is used to serve and thus enliven and embolden the weak, the voiceless, the unseen many, the little ones of this earth? "Are you able to drink the cup that I drink, or be baptized with the baptism that I am baptized with?"

"It is not sufficient for anyone, and it does [one] no good to recognize God in [God's] glory and majesty," wrote Martin Luther, "unless [one] recognizes God in the humility and shame of the cross" (*Heidelberg Disputation*, 20). "O God, you made an instrument of shameful death to be for us the means of life," prayed Thomas Cranmer, "grant us to so glory in the cross of Christ, that we may gladly suffer shame and loss for the sake of your Son our Savior Jesus Christ" (*Book of Common Prayer*, p. 220). In the kingdom of Caesar, crucifixion was used to humiliate and silence anyone—anyone—who proposed another kingdom. Is it any surprise, then, that Jesus' proclamation and embodiment of the kingdom of God, a reign of mercy, forgiveness, and liberation for the many, would collide with the imperial kingdom and his countrymen who collaborated with that kingdom, a reign imposed through violence and at the service of the few?

From the waters of the Jordan, Jesus emerged as a public servant. His life was lived openly in the presence of the many. His baptism at the hands of John the Baptist propelled him into public life. Through word and action, he proclaimed the nearness of God's reign, that reign in which the conventional wisdom of his culture, "the world," was critiqued and turned upside down. Yes, sang his mother in another gospel, "[God] has scattered the proud, . . . brought down the powerful . . . and lifted up the lowly; [God] has filled the hungry with good things, and sent the rich away empty" (Luke 1:51-53). His baptism led to his death. Indeed, his death—*his baptism in the cross*— became the sign of the nearness of the reign of God: the mystery of God revealed in suffering, in self-giving love, in abundant forgiveness, in a peace the world of empires could not understand.

Baptism. Reign of God. Word and sign. Gratitude and rejection. Suffering and death. From the Jordan waters he becomes a public figure, one whose life evokes acceptance *and* rejection. Is this not one of the often unspoken dimensions of baptism: that the baptized, too, become public figures, marked by the Spirit, to serve the reign of God as embodied by Jesus, in our world today? And if this is so, would the baptized not expect to be met with gratitude and rejection, delight and misunderstanding, joy and suffering? Would not the manner of life in service to the reign of God—that reign of God which seeps into all dimensions of life—cause others to wonder, question, rejoice, reject, enter, walk away, sing with joy, or even shout with anger?

"I have been learning a beautiful and harsh truth," wrote Oscar Romero, the martyred archbishop of El Salvador. "I have been learning a beautiful and harsh truth, that the Christian faith does not separate us from the world but immerses us in it; that the church, therefore, is not a fortress set apart from the city, but a follower of Jesus who loved, worked, struggled and died in the midst of the city" (*A Martyr's Message of Hope*).

For reflection and discussion

1. Recover, if you can, your childhood understanding of Jesus of Nazareth. As you have grown older, how has that understanding changed? What has prompted such change?

2. For Mark and other New Testament writers, the central proclamation of Jesus was the nearness or advent of the reign of God in human life. In what ways do you think contemporary Christians experience the nearness of the reign of God today?

3. One claim made in this chapter is that his baptism marks Jesus not only as the beloved servant of God but also as a public figure. If Christian baptism makes one a "public" agent or representative of Jesus Christ, how does his public ministry serve as a blessing or a challenge for your own living of the baptismal covenant?

4. Baptism bestows one's fundamental identity as a public Christian. Do you think Christians should raise their individual or communal voice in public around questions or issues? In light of your reflection on the life and ministry of Jesus, what issues or concerns merit the public voice or actions of Christians?

2

The Catechism
of Culture

Christians live in their own countries,
yet as people on a journey.
Every foreign land is their native country
and their native land, a country of strangers.

For most Christians in North America, the practice of infant baptism is the primary mode of entrance into the Christian community. While these Christian denominations each offer a slightly different understanding of baptism, they share a common expectation: after the baptism of an infant or child, his or her parents will raise the newly baptized in the Christian faith. "Do you promise to help your children grow in the Christian faith and life?" asks the presider of the child's parents. That expectation is extended when the presider announces the responsibilities entrusted to parents: "to live with [the newly baptized] among God's faithful people, bring them to the word of God and the holy supper, teach them the Lord's Prayer, the Creed, and the Ten Commandments, place in their hands the holy scriptures, and nurture them in faith and prayer" (*Evangelical Lutheran Worship*,

p. 228). After the practice of baptism, the expectation of baptismal formation begins in the home and in the Christian assembly. From the celebration of baptism, there emerges what the ancient church called baptismal catechesis.

Sounding down into the ears

That lovely technical term, "catechesis," is an Anglicized form of the Greek original *katekhesis*, meaning "oral instruction" or "sounding down into the ears." In the early church, many lay women and men were designated as catechists or teachers who supervised the formation of people preparing for baptism. Those in preparation for Christian initiation were and continue to be called "catechumens," persons capable of hearing and grasping instruction concerning the three central elements of Christian faith and life: worship (*leitourgia*), study (*didascalia*), and service (*diakonia*). Early Christians frequently baptized individual adults and entire households—parents, children, and servants—with the intention of drawing converts away from the gods, values, and practices of the larger culture and into the living Christ alive in his body, the church. We rarely find evidence of what some would call "indiscriminate baptism"; that is, the practice of baptizing any child or adult with no accompanying formation or catechesis. For the ancient church, it was almost inconceivable that one would be baptized and then communed without some grasp of what was being "put to death" and what was being "raised to new life" in the word and washing of baptism. When our ancestors in the faith read Paul's interpretation of baptism as the death of the old person and a rising of the new person (Rom. 6:1-11), they recognized what contemporary North American Christians frequently overlook: *one entered the process of dying to those values and practices of a culture that were opposed to the values and practices of the gospel of Jesus Christ.* Indeed, one was being raised from the baptismal waters into a new and striking way of perceiving and living in the reality of daily life within one's culture.

When, in 381, the Roman and Christian emperor Theodosius made Christianity the religion of the state, the tension between a minority church and a dominant culture relaxed and began to diminish. What emerged was a reality in which one's ethnic identity as a Greek, an Anglo-Saxon, a Spaniard, or a German came to be associated with one's religious identity. Indeed, while there remained resistance from some Christian bishops to the legalization and imperialization of the church throughout the fifth and sixth centuries, by the early Middle Ages infant baptism had become the normal *religious* practice in all *political* territories governed by Christian rulers. If early Christians usually practiced baptismal catechesis *prior* to baptism, medieval and reformation Christians used a "catechism" to practice baptismal catechesis *after* baptism. To be born English, Norwegian, Italian, or Polish was to be baptized promptly after birth with the expectation that the rest of life would be a sort of baptismal catechesis, a growing into one's baptism at the very same time that one was growing into one's civic or ethnic identity. In this respect, then, it was hard to distinguish Christian faith and life from, for instance, Danish or Scottish or Estonian life. Indeed, the history of immigration to North America testifies to the assimilation of Christianity into various ethnic or national identities: Norwegian Lutherans, English Anglicans, Swiss Calvinists, Italian Roman Catholics, French Huguenots, Orthodox Russians. For hundreds of years of Christian history, one's "culture" supported one's "faith," and this connection, while perhaps not as strong as it once was, has not yet expired.

Of course there are some Christians in North America, as well as other parts of the world, who believe that an authentic mark of the "true" Christian is the determination to transform the state into a "Christian" nation, ruled by biblical law and the ministerial interpreters of that law. And, on the other hand, there are Christians who imagine that to be baptized poses no tension between the larger culture and the gospel of Jesus Christ. For the latter group, one can engage in post-baptismal catechesis with no worry that such cate-chesis will raise a single question about the differences between the gods, values, and practices of Christianity and the culture in which the newly baptized person lives. While infants and adults may be baptized and catechized into "Christian faith and life," those charged with their baptismal formation can overlook or dismiss this salient reality: the dominant culture has already been catechizing them in certain values and practices alien to the gospel of Jesus Christ.

While our recent Christian ancestors might have been able to rely on some degree of cultural support for Christian life, that reliance is no longer possible.

> Today we live in an environment where the Christian church must argue and witness and compete for its place in the life and culture of human beings. Unlike established folk churches from the time of Constantine in the fourth century through the Reformation of the sixteenth century and through the religious revivals of the nineteenth century, the church in North America today has no social and economic privilege and prerogative to extend to its members. Rather, it can offer only Christ and the fellowship of his suffering and the power of his resurrection (*Welcome to Christ*, p. 9).

While Christians in North America might be surrounded by many Christian churches, schools, and agencies, it would be naïve for them to assume that there is broad cultural support for particular Christian traditions and communities. Maybe such support was alive in nineteenth century immigrant communities who shared a common ethnicity and religion. But such is not the case at the beginning of the twenty-first century.

The catechesis of North American culture

In our cultural context, where we enjoy freedom of religion from state interference and where religions of infinite variety can sprout up like wild flowers, Christians can easily miss the tension between Christian baptismal formation and the pervasive and persuasive "catechesis" of North American culture. Such a tension can come as a surprise to many Christians if they imagine that culture and Christianity are two overlapping and complementary dimensions of one's existence, one reinforcing the other. Oh, that it were so simple.

While early Christians were acutely aware of the difference between the catechesis of the Good Shepherd and the "catechesis" of the Roman emperors (the sporadic persecutors of Christians), the difference between Christian life and cultural influence only became prominent again in the twentieth century. Thus, many contemporary biblical scholars, historians, and theologians suggest that the culture we inhabit on a daily basis is not simply a network of passive or neutral influences that float in the air as if one could consciously choose to pick this or that benign influence, as if the culture whose values and practices we breathe in and out every day are "simply there." To the contrary, the culture inhabited by all Christians and all persons coming to Christian faith is a powerful shaper of one's experience, understanding, and interpretation of life. This is to suggest that powerful cultural forces, which many if not most people take for granted and accept as "normal" (such as the economy, the legal system, the entertainment industry, the media), wield considerable influence in shaping human thoughts and feelings, practices and values: "The culture that shapes our hearts has identifiable roots in social forces that control our perceptions and, as in the case of advertising, do so with deliberate skill and foresight" (*Clashing Symbols*, p. 129). What, for instance, is the function of the advertising which inundates us every day in newspapers, billboards, bus ads, radio, magazines, television, and the Internet: to offer objectively constructed information about life in the world? Hardly. Such advertising seeks to create a "need" for a "product" without which one cannot live well in the "modern" world. Additionally, a product which will soon "go out of style" so that another wave of products might be purchased and used. Thus, we are born into a matrix of cultural messages—a catechesis—which, from birth, is continually shaping our understandings of self, others, this world, our purpose, and our meaning in life.

The Irish theologian, Michael Gallagher, notes that the "catechesis" of North American culture (and, he would add, Western European culture) is a particularly powerful force in the lives of young people. This catechesis is filled with messages that invite children and young people to imitate various lifestyles, messages that seek to shape their growing imaginations. What forms the "curriculum" of this cultural catechesis? For one, the needs of the *individual* or the individual's immediate family trump all others. We live in a culture where meeting one's needs and wants holds considerable if not consummate value. Indeed, most of us do not wake up in the morning and ask this first question of the day, "How will we serve the common good?" Hooking up and hanging out are transitory moments of connection in a world where the isolated self increasingly becomes a cultural norm. And yet "getting to the top" by oneself is such a lonely and often treacherous venture (Who is competing for the position?), for when one is "at the top," one is virtually alone with the self, deprived of the support and challenge provided by other human beings. Indeed, a good number of Christian cultural commentators note that North Americans are persuasively formed in egoist tendencies of self-concern and narcissism. If self-giving is at all present in one's imagination, it is increasingly viewed as an episodic experience of voluntarism rather than a habit of the heart. Is this a Christian sensibility: "I am or need to be the center of the universe?" No wonder contemporary African Christians consider North America a missionary territory: "You seem to be losing the deeply human and Christian capacity to be together and help each other over the long haul as imperfect and struggling people," said a well-known Christian bishop from Africa at the end of his recent visit to the United States.

At the same time, North Americans are catechized into relationships marked by aggressive *competition*. Indeed, to gain capital—the goal of a capitalist economy—one must compete vigorously with others in order to "beat them" at the game. Television programs repeatedly highlight this normative practice when they focus on the elimination of contestants in reality shows where "losers" are eliminated weekly and the "winner" eventually takes home the monetary prize because he or she has been skilled in "beating out" the other. Is this a Christian sensibility: one wins and the many fail? In such an "economy," a few will always win and thus be culturally approved or justified by virtue of their hard work, endurance, educational levels, and connections. Such a culturally formed perception of "success" is remarkably powerful in North America, a perception which tends to assign moral value to financial gain and security: monetary comfort (the middle class dream) or manifest wealth (the upper class reality) is often readily interpreted as a sign of blessing from Fate or from God. How easy it is to imagine that one is justified in the sight of others by one's hard work or plain good luck.

At the same time, there is another and even darker dimension to this cultural formation. As Gallagher points out, young women and men—along with their parents and grandparents—are formed in the catechesis of *commodification*. That is, in a consumer economy, in which each person is told repeatedly that one's fundamental purpose is to consume products, the person begins to understand herself or himself as the passive recipient of a seemingly endless array of things. No wonder some churches look like religious supermarkets offering a variety of worship "styles" to suit *culturally-controlled* "tastes" with a diversity of consumable "products" that range from wine or grape juice in tiny glasses or larger cups served with little round wafers, rice crackers, or fragments of bread which can be eaten or dunked in juice or wine. Where a culture of entertainment meets an economy of consumable products, it would seem that every consumer taste must be met.

Even darker is the subtle but real notion that one's identity is found in commodities and that, in the end, *one is a commodity*: a credit card number or a piece of data without a soul, an imagination, or a mind. One has become "objectified" in order to serve the larger goal of selling product and making a profit. In the cultural "catechism" of individualism, consumerism, and entertainment, the individual and the family becomes the passive object of forces committed solely to the acquisition of capital, forces nonetheless which actively and tenaciously form perceptions of the self, others, the world, human meaning, and human purpose. Is this a Christian sensibility: one's fundamental destiny in life is to consume passively an array of goods simply because they are there for the taking or be entertained into passivity while others decide one's fate? Does not Christian faith claim that one's deepest identity is that of a *subject* beloved by God regardless of one's merits, works, or luck; a living subject endowed with an eternal dignity bestowed by God through Christ; a subject who is freed from the need to constantly justify oneself so that one can live in the freedom of service to one's brother or sister, the vulnerable ones among us?

An ancient yet contemporary catechesis

Our early Christian ancestors recognized the almost overwhelming power of their cultures' convictions and practices that, many times, were at odds with the gospel of Jesus Christ. They asked adults or the parents of children to be baptized to recognize clearly that *their lives would not be the same* as they died to old gods, values, and practices in the waters of the font. They asked them to recognize that their lives would not be the same as they were raised to life with Christ in his body, the church, and into service in the world among those deemed the least productive and valuable in the kingdom of Caesar. Is it any wonder, then, that Luther began his catechism with instruction on the Ten Commandments: there are to be no other gods worshiped by the Christian—not the gods of one's imagination nor of one's culture? Here is the first thing our ancient Christian ancestors would have us recognize: life in Christ and his body, the church, is an astonishing gift of grace that no one can achieve, merit, or deserve. Yet held in tension with the gracious offering of baptism is this second thing our ancestors would have us recognize: you are washed into life with Christ and his presence among all the suffering of this world. Is this where you want your life poured out? There is the gift and there is the word of caution, of warning: your life will be forever changed.

Is it any different for North Americans at the beginning of the twenty-first century? Are we so naïve as to assume that formation in a cultural "curriculum" is utterly compatible with the gospel of Jesus Christ? Or is one much-needed focus in baptismal formation bringing the baptized to awareness of the dimensions of this culture which conflict with the gospel of Jesus Christ? How should leaders alert young people, parents of newly baptized infants or children, and prospective members or catechumens to the ways in which some cultural forces play persuasively on the imagination and shape one's sense of self, others, human purpose, God, salvation, community, ethics? Or will pastors, catechists, bishops, teachers, priests, preachers, deacons, and other congregational leaders—so concerned about the minority status of their church bodies in North America—raise not one troubling question or speak a critical word for fear that prospective members might walk out the door and current members might bolt? Perhaps, then, congregational leaders need to remember this salient point: Jesus of Nazareth was not crucified because his mission and manner of life complemented the culture of his time. He would not have endured withering criticism from religious critics and the public humiliation of a political execution had his "good news" been no more than a recipe for escaping life in this world. Indeed, *no one is crucified because they support the status quo; and no one is raised from the dead to return to the way things have always been.*

When leaders of Christian or baptismal formation meet with young people, parents of infants or children about to be baptized, and adults seeking baptism, they can imagine that their purpose is to present persuasively the central convictions and practices of the faith, to make the faith "appealing" to others. As Paul Tillich, the German American theologian, noted in his letter to Christian ministers and teachers, it is impossible to make the Christian message appealing (*Theology of Culture*, p. 201). Why? Quite simply yet profoundly, the Christian message asks for a death, a death to an old way of living in this world with the self alone at the center. One cannot transform the Christian message and way of life into a "product" to be marketed since *it ushers one into a life where trust in God and love for the neighbor in need are at the center*. In service to that tension, that daily dying of the self shaped by larger cultural forces, one can ask questions which may help the catechumen, the parent, and the spiritual seeker recognize the difference between "cultural catechesis" and the promise of baptismal formation. One can ask: *Who is imaging your life for you and asking you to accept such images of life*? Such a question may come as a surprise to the person who thinks that he or she is "creating" a life on their own. The question, of course, brings to awareness that we are born and raised in a culture where others, often powerful others, are asking us to accept images of ourselves shaped by cultural hyper-individualism, aggressive competition, and passive commodification.

Or the catechist, pastor, or baptismal sponsor may ask: *Who is telling you stories that claim to show reality*? Given the powerful claim on the imagination by the film and television industries, such a question asks one to consider other narratives which show us how we might live in this world. For instance, young children have access to video games in which they play soldiers who can blow off the head, arms, or legs, fatally puncture the stomach, or disfigure the face of an "enemy" soldier. Is this a story—an imagined role—that we would want to shape a child's imagination? Is it not an enactment of violence seemingly incompatible with the nonviolent Jesus into whom the child was baptized? While we may ask others if they "liked" or "disliked" a video game, a film, or a television show, such a question completely misses the point: an engaging and moving visual narrative works subconsciously on the imagination and fills it with images, wonderful or terrifying, of life and relationships in this world. This is not to say that such media per se are at odds with the gospel of Jesus Christ. Indeed, many reveal dimensions of grace, suffering, forgiveness, the tragic consequences of greed and pride, restoration, unexpected mercy, enlightenment, and healing found in the biblical, sacramental, and theological traditions of Christians. And yet baptismal formation—prior to or after the sacramental celebration—rightly asks the question, *Who is telling you stories,* and points to other narratives, biblical and historical narratives, which reveal a reality shaped by God's grace and mercy, a diverse, fragile, and life-giving creation, a redemption which liberates from enslavement and diminishment, and a way of living in this world shaped by "serving all people, following the example of Jesus, and striving for justice and peace in all the earth" (*Evangelical Lutheran Worship*, p. 236; *Book of Common Prayer*, p. 305).

Ancient Christian ancestors asked those about to be baptized to face the west, where the sun descends into darkness, as they renounced "the devil and all his works, the world and all its vain pleasures." In one of his sermons on baptism, the fourth-century bishop Ambrose of Milan asked the newly baptized to "be mindful of your words of renunciation and never let the contents of this bond pass from your memory." In turn, the catechumens faced the east, where sun brings light into the world, as they professed their faith in "God the Father almighty, in our Lord Jesus Christ and in his cross, and in the Holy Spirit." The first turning of the body and the words of renunciation, the second turning of the body and the words of confession—together these words and actions marked the tension which would accompany the baptized throughout their lives: a dying to the old order of this world and a rising to the new order of Jesus Christ. It is easy to overlook the tension and let it collapse into unwarranted hate for *or* naïve acceptance of this world and the power of its cultures. Christians are called to live within the tension between two dynamics: "God so loved the world that he gave his only Son" (John 3:16) and "Do not be conformed to this world" (Rom. 12:2). It is easy to let the tension relax. It is more difficult and invigorating to live within the two: love for this world and resistance to its conforming power.

For reflection and discussion

1. When in your life have you experienced a palpable tension between the gospel of Jesus Christ and the values or practices of the larger culture in which you live? What is one point of tension or conflict and why is it significant for you?

2. We would be wrong to imagine that North American culture has no value or good to offer Christians. What do you consider one or two cultural values or practices which support or even rightly challenge Christians in their faith and life?

3. For close to two hundred years in North America, one's ethnic heritage served as the "holder" of one's religious identity: one could safely assume that Danish immigrants were Lutheran and Italian immigrants, Roman Catholic. But in the increasingly pluralistic cultures of North America, the relationship between ethnicity and religious identity has started to unravel. And increasingly people enter churches with no familial or ethnic formation in faith and life. Does this assessment reflect your experience? If so, what challenges does it bring?

4. Preparation for the baptism of infants or adults can frequently focus on the "spiritual" responsibilities of parents or what the church "believes" and offers adults. This chapter has asked that one *first* consider the powerful influence of North American culture in shaping desires, relationships with others, and expectations of the self and religion. What do you consider one powerful way in which the larger culture erodes the baptismal sense of community, "bearing each other's burdens," and genuine human relationships with those who are quite different from oneself?

5. The reform movements of the sixteenth century asked troubling questions about that which most people took for granted. Becoming *aware* that one's expectations of life or self-understanding or relationships is being shaped, often subtly, by others can be a surprising awareness for some people. In your reflection on this chapter, what questions have emerged?

6. What would you consider to be one or two gifts which Christians can offer to people who have been shaped by toxic individualism, aggressive competition, and increasing commodification of humans and human relationships?

3
Entering and Leaving the Water

Anyone who comes to me
I will never drive away.

For many North Americans, affiliation with a religious group is perceived in a very American way: as a voluntary and private act, made by the individual, which introduces one to a group of other individuals who elect to gather on a regular basis for "religious" activities. Thus, the way one enters a religious community is shaped, to some degree, by a cultural perception of religion: a conscious decision by the individual, in conversation with a religious professional, which leads to a public acknowledgement of this emerging affiliation. Becoming a Christian may entail a number of conversations with a pastoral leader or participation in a "newcomers" class followed by a baptism celebrated in the middle of the Sunday liturgy. For parents of infants to be baptized, the process may look little different: a few conversations or classes followed by a Sunday baptism. In either case, preparation for baptism may be an orderly experience but a brief one focused on the communication of information about the local church, a parent's responsibilities for a child, or the distinctiveness of a particular Christian communion. To say the least, such a contemporary practice stands in contrast to early Christian practices. One ancient source narrates baptismal preparation in this manner:

> As many as are persuaded and believe that what we teach and say is true, and undertake to be able to live accordingly, are taught to pray and to ask God, with fasting, for the forgiveness of their past sins. We pray and fast with them. Then they are brought by us where there is water, and are reborn in the same manner in which we ourselves were reborn (Justin Martyr, *Apology*, 61).

A second source offers a more distinctly detailed description of this preparation:

> Those who are to be initiated into the new faith are first brought to the catechists to hear the word. They are to be asked the reason why they seek the faith. [Their sponsors] shall testify regarding their capacity to hear the word. They are to be asked about their state of life . . . and their trades and professions. If the person is a [pimp] . . . a gladiator . . . a guardian of idols . . . a soldier who imposes the death penalty . . . a prostitute . . . a fortune-teller . . . a man with a concubine—they are to give it up or be sent away. They are to listen to the word for three years [but a shorter time may be appropriate] . . . They are to pray together and the catechist is to lay hands on them and pray for them . . . [As they prepare for baptism], their life is to be examined: have they respected widows and visited the sick? As the day of their baptism approaches, the bishop is to pray over them . . . On Friday and Saturday before their baptism, they are to fast . . . On Saturday, the bishop prays with them and makes the sign of the cross on their bodies . . . The water is to be flowing . . . The candidates are to remove

their clothes, the children baptized first, then the men, then the women (Hippolytus of Rome, *The Apostolic Tradition*, 15-21).

Formation for Christian faith and life

While Hippolytus narrates a process marked by his more stringent ethical sensibilities, he and Justin attest to a baptismal preparation which takes place over a period of time and is focused on communal worship and prayer, study of scripture, and service to the vulnerable and the poor. Catechists, sponsors, other Christians, clergy, and the bishop accompany those preparing for baptism. It is a preparation accomplished in and with *the entire community of the baptized* who, as Justin notes, "pray and fast with them." It is a baptismal preparation which *asks serious questions*: is it possible for one who uses, abuses, or kills another to live the Christian life? Who is at the center of one's life: the emperor, other gods and idols, the starry Fates, or the God of Jesus Christ? It is a process which *takes time*, an undetermined amount of time or a process marked by the seasons of the church year. From these early Christian sources, it appears that one does not rush into baptism—yes, one does not rush to the font.

While many well-intentioned contemporary churches strain to be as open, welcoming, and attractive as possible, early Christians took a decidedly different stance. They asked serious questions. They involved others in the preparation process. They were patient. They studied the scriptures together. Perhaps they were inspired by the New Testament story of an encounter between an African man and Philip, an evangelist:

> Now there was an Ethiopian eunuch, a court official of the Candace, queen of the Ethiopians, in charge of her entire treasury. He had come to Jerusalem to worship and was returning home; seated in his chariot, he was reading the prophet Isaiah. Then the Spirit said to Philip, "Go over to this chariot and join it." So Philip ran up to it and heard him reading the prophet

> Isaiah. He asked, "Do you understand what you are reading?" He
> replied, "How can I, unless someone guides me?" And he invited
> Philip to get in and sit beside him ... The eunuch asked Philip,
> "About whom, may I ask you, does the prophet say this, about
> himself or about someone else?" Then Philip began to speak,
> and starting with this scripture, he proclaimed to him the good
> news about Jesus. As they were going along the road, they came
> to some water; and the eunuch said, "Look, here is water! What is
> to prevent me from being baptized?" He commanded the chariot
> to stop, and both of them, Philip and the eunuch, went down
> into the water, and Philip baptized him (Acts 8:27-31, 34-38).

Here we see one person coming to another and, thus, a small community, a little church, is formed, "for where two or three are gathered in my name, I am there among them" (Matt. 18:20). Questions are asked and a request is made for guidance from another. They sit together and Philip, the catechist, begins to show him how the scriptures point to and reveal the good news of Jesus Christ. They do not simply read the Bible together but discuss its meaning for the life of the Ethiopian, himself a person of ambiguous sexuality who, as a eunuch, would be excluded from some religious communities. Time is spent in reflection "as they were going along the road." Then the Ethiopian candidate asks for baptism, and Philip baptizes him. In this brief early Christian story, we may recognize, in a microcosm, the apprenticeship in faith and life which is expanded a century later in the testimony of Justin and Hippolytus. What we recognize in the story, which appears to happen in one afternoon, is the emergence of a longer process for adults who wish to become Christian.

Or perhaps early Christians were inspired by Jesus' instructions to his disciples as narrated in the Gospel of Matthew:

> Now the eleven disciples went to Galilee, to the mountain
> to which Jesus had directed them. When they saw him, they

worshiped him; but some doubted. And Jesus came and said to them, "All authority in heaven and on earth has been given to me. Go therefore and make disciples of all nations, baptizing them in the name of the Father and of the Son and of the Holy Spirit, and teaching them to obey everything that I have commanded you. And remember, I am with you always, to the end of the age" (Matt. 28:16-20).

Matthew points to the relationship between teaching and baptism: adults receive teaching or formation in faith *prior to baptism*; infants and young children receive teaching or formation in faith *after baptism*. While the New Testament offers no blueprint for teaching or formation, there are hints and glimpses sufficient enough to recognize key elements. Early Christian preparation prior to or following baptism includes ongoing guidance by the Christian community and its leaders (e.g., evangelists, catechists, pastors or presbyters, sponsors, the bishop, the worshiping assembly). There is time for questions and conversation, formation in the scriptures, learning to pray and worship as Christians, and service among those in need. In other words, what one recognizes emerging in the New Testament and blossoming into an orderly pattern of baptismal preparation are the very marks of Christian life: worship, study, and service within a community of faith.

Baptismal welcome into a minority community

The historic Christian communions in North America have begun to experience what early Christians took for granted: our status as a minority religion among the many religions and value systems of the dominant culture. Contemporary American Christians may read Justin and Hippolytus and then conclude that much time, perhaps too much time, was spent on preparing people for baptism. Eager to welcome people into churches whose membership is returning to pre–World War II numbers, some contemporary North Americans may be simply baffled that months if not a year or more could be spent in conversation, discernment, prayer, study, worship, and service—an apprenticeship in Christian faith and life. Yet early Christians may have something to teach modern Christians: baptismal identity is not simply one more "addition" to a life in which being Christian competes with being a citizen, a consumer, a worker, a parent, a spouse, and a friend. Instead, one's baptismal identity means that one's life will be changed and changed significantly forever. Thus, early Christians offered a clear word of caution or warning at the beginning of baptismal preparation: you will die to a life focused solely on the self and will be raised into a life of faith in God and service to your neighbor in need. You will begin to live within the tension between two impulses: "God so loved the world that he gave his only Son" (John 3:16) and "Do not be conformed to this world" (Rom. 12:2). Indeed, your life will be shaped by the One who emptied himself of every claim to power over others and became their servant (Phil. 2:7). Living into that word of caution, that life-changing worldview, and that real tension form part of the fabric of baptismal preparation.

While many early Christians clearly experienced and taught that the new life in Christ is an unmerited gift of God and a gracious means of incorporation into the body of Christ, they also understood that life in Christ was lived by persons who constituted a minority within the larger culture. They recognized clearly the tension between loving this world created by God and resisting those "trades and professions" which symbolized the power of the strong to crush the weak and the desire to use others as objects for one's economic gain or personal pleasure. They recognized that one's destiny was not tied to Fate or the stars but to the Creator and Redeemer.

As a minority community, early Christians would have contemporary Christians recognize that initial formation in faith—"teaching leading to baptism"—places the seeker, the catechumen, the Christian within a vision of life in this world shaped by the gospel of Jesus Christ. That gospel is not one extra addition, one more compartment of life to be accessed a few hours each week or when trouble hits. Rather, the gospel bestows a different way of seeing, thinking, and living in this world. Thus, one of the primary purposes of baptismal preparation for adults or parents of children is to welcome them into this alternative vision of life with the Holy Three, in a community of faithful servants, within this world. In this regard, early Christians welcomed Jews and Gentiles, males and females, slaves and the wealthy into their communities through baptism. They crossed ethnic, gender, and socioeconomic distinctions with an inclusive baptismal practice. For in the cross of Jesus, no one could or can claim privilege based on gender, race, or status. No one "deserves" or has a "right" to what is freely offered by God in Christ through the water washing of baptism. Indeed, baptismal preparation itself is no project, work, or process that merits the grace of baptism. "It cannot be understood as a 'work' we do in order to 'climb up' to God" (*Welcome to Christ*, p. 53).

One wonders: were early Christians aware that a brisk or episodic baptismal preparation would lead to a shallow sense of Christian faith and life? Did they sense that conversion to Christ and his gospel was a radical transformation of one's mind and affections, an ongoing transformation that would result in a distinctive manner of life? Did they want to offer as much assistance as possible, as much time as was needed for those who, Justin writes, "are persuaded and believe that what we teach and say is true, and undertake to be able to live accordingly"? Did they recognize with utter clarity what contemporary Christians may sometimes overlook: That a sustained initial formation in the community of the baptized truly shapes one's affections, thinking, and commitments? That formation in worship and prayer, the scriptures, and service in daily life honestly present the three marks of ongoing Christian life? That time is needed for questions, conversation, reflection on scripture, learning to pray as Christians pray, and recognizing that all visitors and seekers, life-long Christians, children, bishops, catechists, infants, pastors, parents—whoever joins the assembly for worship—are *beggars*, standing with open hands together before God as revealed in the gospel of Jesus Christ? That no one "has arrived," and that no one has plumbed "the depths of God" (Job 11:7)?

Baptism leading to formation in faith

While early Christians commonly baptized entire families—"the candidates are to remove their clothes, the children baptized first, then the men, then the women"—medieval and reformation Christians focused baptismal practice on infants. Thus, the linking of "teaching and baptism" was reversed: the baptism of infants was followed by a formation in faith that was intended to take place throughout life until one's death. Indeed, parents and the local community were and are charged with the formation of infants and young children. Consequently, the catechisms of the sixteenth-century reformers set forth a pattern of baptismal preparation corresponding to early Christian sources: learning the commandments which focus on the "love and trust of God above all things" and the "help and support" offered one's neighbors; coming to faith in the Holy Three as set forth in the Creed; formation in prayer, in particular, the Lord's Prayer; and entering into the practice and meanings of Holy Baptism and the Holy Eucharist.

By the third and fourth centuries, many early Christians maintained what scholars call a unitary baptismal practice—water-washing, hand-laying with prayer, and a first communion of children and adults. The sixteenth-century reformers, however, received a divided practice: water-washing of infants was separated, by seven to nine years, from hand-laying (what came to be called "confirmation") and communion at the supper. Thus, "confirmation classes" developed as a preparation for a young person's public affirmation of his or her baptism as an infant. This medieval practice, continued by the reformers, has endured in the many churches of the reformation. Yet the practice of holding "classes" for teenagers can miss the larger picture: baptism as an adult or as an infant welcomes one into *lifelong formation in faith.* The baptized Christian is nourished and challenged in Christian identity through participation in word and sacrament—the liturgy of the Sunday assembly—and the invitation to serve one's neighbor as a member of the priestly people of God. Indeed, when contemporary Christians focus on episodic moments of teaching or formation in faith—a few enquiry or confirmation classes—one can readily receive the impression that the life of faith is itself episodic or that one can "graduate" out of formation. How can there be a moment when a congregation or parish has offered "enough" formation in faith for infants, their parents, adult newcomers, or teenagers? Perhaps western Christians can learn from Eastern Christians who continue to baptize and commune infants. There is no separate "confirmation" that coincides with reaching puberty or the "age of reason." There is only the expectation and the promise that the rest of one's life will be shaped by ongoing formation in faith through worship and prayer, study of scripture, and service to others in daily life.

Such a focus can alter a vision of congregational or parish life. If a community of faith lives from and organizes itself first as a center of baptismal and eucharistic practice and formation and thus as an assembly focused on formation for witness and service in daily life, then the profound relationships between worship and witness, formation and service, gospel and mission become living realities rather than separated or abstract "notions" of what constitutes congregational life. Thus, the purpose of "teaching and baptism" is not to form a closed, therapeutic community which tells only its many little personal "stories." Rather, baptismal formation rightly juxtaposes one's personal story with the story of scripture and asks, "How does this other story, the story of God's creative and redeeming work in human lives, cause us to reinterpret the personal or family story?" Nor is the purpose of "baptism and teaching" to form an extroverted entrepreneurial community set on "recruiting" new members, as if the purpose of the church is to keep pace with mortality rates or succumb to the American expectation that growth in numbers is evidence of success or providential blessing. Rather, baptismal formation rightly focuses on the gospel alternative to the cultural measurement of "success"—a measurement in which some always win and some always lose.

As communities of faith who have virtually no social or economic advantages, no status or privileges to extend to others, faithful baptismal formation can offer only Jesus Christ, the fellowship of his suffering love for this world, and the power of his resurrection present in human lives. Early Christians called this "offering," this invitation to be joined to the dead and risen Jesus Christ, *the paschal mystery*: It is our Passover with him, through the water-washing of baptism, into a new way of seeing, thinking, and relating to God, each other, and this world. It is our invitation to live with the constant tension between a world in which the "I" is at the center and the world in which the Holy Three and the neighbor pull us outward—in trusting faith toward God and in love toward one's neighbors. This tension suggests that the path to and from Jordan's stream, the font, is marked by daily conversions, for we are not yet what we shall be.

> This life is, therefore,
> not righteousness but growth in righteousness
> not health but healing,
> not being but becoming
> not rest but exercise.
> We are not yet what we shall be,
> but we are growing toward it.
> The process is not yet finished
> but it is going on.
> This is not the end
> but it is the road.
> All does not yet gleam with glory
> but all is being purified.
>
> —Martin Luther
> *Defense and Explanation of All the Articles*, 2

For reflection and discussion

1. Is baptismal preparation on the collective "radar screen" of your congregation, or is it a process in which only a few people participate? Is there consistent preaching and teaching about baptism and baptismal preparation in your congregation? Do your congregational members view *themselves* as a baptismal or catechumenal congregation?

2. As Tertullian, an early Christian teacher, once wrote: people are not "born" Christian but are "made" Christian in the baptismal font— and how they are "made" or formed in Christian faith and life matters enormously. Brisk or "efficient" baptismal preparation can fail to honor the questions and expectations curious people bring and can be a disservice to the richness of Christian faith and life. What is one way in which baptismal preparation might be strengthened in your setting?

3. While there are congregations and church bodies which are quick to trumpet "mission" or "God's mission" as their central purpose, such terms can also mask the anxiety some church leaders and members share as mainline churches decline in numbers. Is it possible that preparing people to live and serve in a minority religion for the long haul might be a more appropriate use of one's resources and gifts? To follow the witness of early Christians, might a more robust form of baptismal welcome, preparation, celebration, and lifelong formation enable Christian communities to release their anxiety and joyously embrace their minority status?

4
The Many Meanings
of Christian Baptism

Fountain of grace, rich, full, and free.
What need I, that is not in thee?
Full pardon, strength to meet the day.
And peace which none can take away.

At the center of the northern Italian city of Milan, one will find the great Piazza del Duomo, the plaza in front of the cathedral church. Built between the fourteenth and sixteenth centuries, the current cathedral building is the largest Gothic structure in Italy, surrounded by an open space built over the ancient imperial forum. It wasn't until construction began on a twentieth-century subway system that an earlier church and baptismal hall, dating from the fourth century, were discovered underneath the cathedral piazza. In this earlier baptismal hall, with a font some ten feet in width, Ambrose of Milan, the city's bishop, baptized Augustine of Hippo, in 387. While he supervised the preparation of baptismal candidates and preached numerous sermons on the significance of baptism, Ambrose also composed and then had this inscription placed on the wall of the hall, above the octagonal, eight-sided, baptismal font:

> This hall of eight walls rises here for a holy purpose:
> the octagonal font is a noble holder of God's gift.
> It was right that on the number eight
> the hall of sacred baptism should rise
> in which true salvation is given to all in the light of the risen
>   Christ.
> It is he who opens the prison of death, wakes the lifeless from
>   the tomb,
> and washes them in the current of the pure-flowing font,
> freeing from the power of sin those who have already confessed
>   their guilt.
>
> For all those who want to abandon the sins of a former life,
> let their hearts be washed here and find their minds restored.
> Let them come quickly and not hesitate for a moment:
> those who approach and are washed leave whiter than snow.
> Let the saints come to the font and be washed in the kingdom
>   of God.
> O the glory of God's justice!
> For what is more divine and more just than this:
> that in a brief instant the guilt of a people crumbles and
>   is washed away?

An ardent student of the scriptures, Ambrose knew that the first creation account in Genesis (1:1—2:3) speaks of seven days of creation. For many early Christians, Ambrose among them, baptism not only made a person Christian, it also ushered in a new perception of time: an "eighth" and unending "day"—one that began with Christ's resurrection from the dead. For these early Christians, the power of his resurrection was not limited to one moment in time. Rather, the resurrection of Christ from the finality of human death opened time for all who participate in the resurrection through baptism. They are washed into a new creation and new sense of time which moves beyond death. Thus baptism into Christ's risen life initiates the newly baptized into a time which has no end. Consequently, the baptismal hall, built as an octagon enclosing an eight-sided font, was a visual symbol of this new sense of time, the "eighth day" which has no end. The building and its large baptismal pool welcomed people into the risen life of Christ, a life with an open horizon.

Always more than one meaning, one word

This ancient inscription also reveals another sensibility among our ancient spiritual ancestors: there is always more than one meaning, one effect, one way of experiencing and understanding baptism. The ambrosian inscription speaks of the baptismal ritual as receiving a gift, being enlightened, opening a closed door, waking from lifelessness, washing in fresh water, being freed from oppressive powers, restoring one's mind, and cleansing from and forgiving of sin. Notice how the images seem to pile up, one next to the other, as if the meaning of baptism could never be contained in one word or image, as if baptism contained a surplus of meanings, each one illuminating the diverse power and presence of baptism in the lives of the baptized. Indeed, other early Christian inscriptions speak of baptism as being marked by the hand of the Good Shepherd, being washed in the wounds of Christ, receiving the cross, birthing from the womb of the church, and life-giving washing of the whole world.

Early Christian baptismal fonts, large enough for the full immersion of one or more adults, were built into the earth in a variety of shapes: some square, some round, some octagonal, some cruciform, some many-lobed or labial—each shape another symbolic expression of baptism's meanings. For instance, a labial-shaped font could suggest a birth from the womb of the Spirit or the church. A cross-shaped font could indicate a tomb or watery grave—a death to a former way of life or being washed in the wounds of Christ. An octagonal font might welcome one into the eighth day of risen life with Christ, and a rounded font—a ring without end or beginning—communicates the eternal, unending gift of life received in baptism. Where fonts are decorated with fish, animals, birds, trees, flowers, and fruits, baptism becomes an entrance into Paradise, once lost to Adam and now restored in Christ, the second or "new" Adam. Thus, the very shape of the font could signal a womb, a grave, an open future, an eternal ring, or a fertile garden. Rather than reduce the meaning of baptism to one action or one image or one word, it would seem that early Christians, immersed in the rich imagery of the Bible, were not content with a minimalist approach to the meaning of baptism: only forgiveness or only death to sin or only birth into the household of faith. The Bible itself would not allow such a narrowing of baptism's power and presence in the life the baptized and the church. Thus, the visual artifacts—inscriptions, baptismal halls, font sizes and shapes, and artwork—communicated the many images of salvation through water present in the Bible.

In its archaic form, baptism may have been practiced as a simple washing in water followed by the community's thanksgiving meal. In the second century, Justin Martyr writes that Christians fast and pray with baptismal candidates who are then "brought by us where there is water, and are reborn in the same manner in which we ourselves were reborn" (*Apology*, 61). Two centuries later, Ambrose presided at and preached about a baptismal practice with slightly richer biblical connotations. Since the Easter Vigil was the primary Christian festival of the ancient church and since baptism was celebrated at the Great Vigil, Ambrose composed a series of sermons, preached throughout Easter Week, that unfolded the various meanings of the ritual actions through which people became Christians. Notice how the biblical texts serve as inspiration for the action or are spoken or sung during the action:

Those to be baptized in the octagonal font at Milan are first touched on the ears and lips as Mark 7:31-37 is read—the story of Jesus opening the ears and lips of a deaf man with a speech impediment. "Let your ears be open to the exhortation of the minister [who will baptize you]," declares Ambrose.

Then turning to the west, the cardinal direction in which the sun sets, the candidates renounce their "adversary," the Evil One and all his powers, and then spit—yes, spit—toward the west and the face of the Evil One who cannot bear the light of Christ. They then turn toward the east, the direction from which the sun emerges, to confess their faith in the Holy Three, the source of light and spiritual enlightenment.

Standing near the font, the candidates are stripped naked as Genesis 2:18-25 (Adam and Eve naked in the garden) or Mark 1:9-11 (Jesus' baptism in the Jordan) is read. Ambrose notes that once the candidate is naked, olive oil is rubbed over the entire body, an action inspired by Paul's description of the Christian life as an athletic race in which runners are first anointed with oil (1 Cor. 9:24-27): "You were rubbed like an athlete, Christ's athlete, as if to contend in this contest of this world," he preached in one of his Easter sermons on baptism.

Thanksgiving then is made to God over the waters and then the candidates are immersed in the pool three times in the name of the Trinity. Concerning the water-washing, Ambrose invokes various biblical images to describe God's work in word and water. At the beginning of creation, God invites the waters to "bring forth swarms of living creatures" (Gen. 1:20). Water generates life, Ambrose writes, but the word and water of God in baptism "regenerate you in grace, just as water generated other creatures unto life. Imitate the fish, which indeed has obtained less grace yet should be an object of wonder to you. . . . Be yourself a fish that the waters of this world may not overwhelm you." Through baptismal washing, God drowns the deathly Adam in all humanity, created from the "dust of the ground" (Gen. 2:7), loosens the grip of the devil and death, and establishes them in the resurrection. In baptism, "you receive the sacrament of the cross . . . you are crucified with Christ; you cling to Christ." Ambrose quotes Paul: "I have been crucified with Christ; and it is no longer I who live, but it is Christ who lives in me" (Gal. 2:19-20). Ambrose continues: "In the flood (Gen. 6:5—8:19), there was a figure of baptism. . . . What is the flood except . . . the seminary of justice where sin dies." Baptismal washing is a passing through the sea, from slavery to the powers of this world into the freedom of the children of God (Exod. 14:1-15). Again he quotes the Apostle: "Our ancestors were all under the cloud, and all passed through the sea, and all were baptized into Moses in the cloud and in the sea" (1 Cor. 10:1-2). Thus, the passage through the Red Sea becomes an image and interpretation of Christian baptism, a saving image poured into the font of Holy Baptism.

But there is more. Drawing from the same narrative, he invokes the story of Moses casting a piece of wood into the bitter water so that the thirsty people might drink from it (Exod. 15:22-25). For Christians, claims Ambrose, the waters of baptism, so sweet and pleasant, now withdraw the bitterness of our mortality. With Naaman the Syrian, suffering with leprosy (2 Kings 5:1-14), the baptismal candidates enter the baptismal pool, the Jordan River, to be healed by Christ who, himself, was baptized in the waters of that river (Matt. 3:13-17). And this: "See the mystery," he writes, "our Lord Jesus Christ comes to the pool (at Bethsaida; John 5:1-18); then says to the paralytic, 'Go down.' Behold you [who have gone down into the font] are baptized from the cross of Christ, from the death of Christ. There is the mystery, because he suffered for you. In him you are redeemed; in him you are saved." In the midst of his preaching, he says: "Behold the incidents in Scripture, one by one." Thus, in his preaching among the newly baptized, in his desire to *open up* rather than reduce the great mystery of baptism, Ambrose places various actions and images around the font: a sea of watery, fertile regeneration in grace; a drowning of mortality inherited from the first Adam; a flood in which sin is washed away; a watery passage into freedom and genuine community; a fountain where one drinks the very life of God; the unexpected gift of healing; a rising with Christ into new and unending life.

The newly baptized then stand before the minister, naked and dripping, as fragrant olive oil is poured or smeared over their heads, in the sign of the cross, while the gifts of the Holy Spirit are invoked: "the spirit of wisdom and understanding, of counsel and might, of knowledge and the fear of the LORD, the spirit of joy" (Isa. 11:2; *Evangelical Lutheran Worship*, p. 231; *Book of Common Prayer*, p. 308). Ambrose then says, "How many souls renewed today love you, Lord Jesus, saying, 'Let us run after you, that we may drink in the odor of your Resurrection,' for Christ gave himself up for us, a fragrant offering to God (Eph. 5:2)." Washed in water and smeared with fragrant oil, the newly baptized are then clothed in a white garment, a white alb, "because the garments of Christ were white as snow when in the gospel he showed the glory of his resurrection (Matt. 17:2)." Invoking the lyrical love poetry of the Song of Solomon, Ambrose suggests that the white robe is also a bridal garment worn by the newly baptized, the beloved, as they are wedded to Christ, the lover: "On seeing his church in white vesture, washed in the pool of regeneration, Christ says: 'Behold, you are fair, my love . . . place me as a seal on your heart' (Song of Sol. 8:6) that your faith may shine with the fullness of the sacrament."

Now sweet-smelling and clothed in white, the newly washed are then led to the altar: "The cleansed people of God, *rich in these insignia*, hasten to the altar of Christ, saying, 'I shall go to the altar of God, the God who gives joy to my youth' (Ps. 42:4)." As the newly baptized come to the Lord's table for their first communion, the people sing Psalm 23: "He prepares a table before me . . . my cup overflows." Christ feeds his church on these sacraments, Ambrose writes, so that the Christian people, like plantings in a fertile garden, might "burst forth into good fruits with a growth of new richness."

Cultural simplification, Christian richness, and human need
Now one might rightly ask: Why did early Christians build such great baptismal halls, celebrate such a rich baptismal ceremony, and spend so much time preaching about, what one scholar calls,

the "awe-inspiring rites of initiation"? What could that ancient Mediterranean practice possibly mean for contemporary American Christians? Wouldn't a sprinkling of water, from a little cup, with the invocation of the Holy Trinity suffice? Don't the baptismal architecture, baptismal practice, and post-baptismal teaching of the early church seem, well, too much? Is all *that* really needed when an efficient practice will suffice? Indeed, Christians have taught that for a "valid" baptism one only need pour the smallest amount of water on the head with the declaration: You are baptized in the name of the Father, Son, and Holy Spirit. What more does one need than that?

Perhaps we should consider that, in addition to robust individualism, aggressive competition, and a tendency to make just about everything—including religion—into a marketable product, North American culture is marked by a preference for *simplification*. Indeed, to compete in a consumer and capitalist marketplace, a product must be mass-marketed so that a third-grader can grasp its purpose and value quickly. On the whole, we are a people who prefer the simple solution, who like to get things "fixed" quickly—a busy people without much time on our hands. While there are exceptions to our love for simplification, on the whole we prefer the magazine to the book, the action-focused movie rather than a slower, character-focused film. Efficiency in action, brevity of message, and simplicity of content rank as strongly desired values in a culture where people are formed by the media in short attention spans. A large building holding an ample baptismal pool? A church service of more than one hour? A ritual with ten actions rather than two? A full week of preaching on one sacrament? In a culture which shapes Christians to ask for less rather than more, for simplification rather than a rich ambiguity, for efficiency rather than complexity, the multimedia celebration of baptism in the ancient church might look, to some, like an overwrought ceremony from another planet.

Ambrose knew something different. The Bible itself is not a "message" which can be reduced to a few one-liners, no matter how attractive such an idea might be to the contemporary marketer. For the

Bible is a rich, multivoiced, at times contradictory, and wonderfully complex witness to a mystery: a mystery that cannot be contained, pinned down, expedited, or simplified for mass market consumption; a mystery burning at the heart of all things; the mystery of God revealed in the flesh; the mystery of God dwelling among humans in ways not even we can yet imagine. While much of contemporary North American culture may reduce religion or Christianity or baptism to a simple slogan and quick ritual, Christians rightly say No to such expectations. Ambrose and his early Christian colleagues did not engage in a practice marked by biblical richness and symbolic, ritual complexity because they had nothing better to do with their time! Rather, they led their congregations in such practices because they knew that *Christian baptism was and is the primal, public, and unrepeatable ensemble of actions and words through which one's public, personal, communal, and eternal identity is bestowed.* How one is "marked as Christ's forever" shapes how one will grow into and be enriched by that marking throughout a lifetime.

Of course a random sprinkling of water with a few words muttered over one's head does, indeed, communicate the promise and presence of God—but does it really communicate the richness of one's new identity, a richness which is intended to accompany the newly baptized throughout life? Or say it this way: Ambrose and other early Christian ministers spent considerable time preaching about the richness of baptism and its many actions because they were acutely aware of the people in their congregations and the needs that people brought to the church. For instance, to the person who is burdened with numbing guilt for the harm he or she has done to another, baptism offers the blessed *forgiveness* of one's sin. As the ambrosian inscription notes, "What is more divine and more just than this: that in a brief instant the guilt of a people crumbles and is washed away?" To another person who is recovering from an addiction, the gift of baptism may well be the *liberation* it promises from oppressive forces, from one's adversary that is bent on dehumanizing God's own creatures. Or this:

baptism may hold forth the gift of *birth* into a new way of living with one's struggles, one's darker tendencies—a way of living with realistic hope for the future in a supportive community. To still another who longs for companionship, baptismal washing and the fellowship of the table offer the bonds of *community*, the royal priesthood of all the baptized. To the person who has experienced his or her social status as something so "low" that one feels invaluable, imagine the invigorating power of being smeared with fragrant oil that proclaims one a *beloved child* of the Most High, a brother or sister of Christ, a king or a queen in the reign of God?

Thus to claim that there is more than one meaning in Christian baptism, more than one effect, more than one gracious gift, is to acknowledge the rich diversity of the New Testament and, at the same time, to recognize that people seeking baptism bring, within themselves, more than one need, dream, burden, or aspiration. When preaching and teaching reduce the gift and promise of baptism to one or two meanings, the inherent richness of the baptismal treasure is overlooked and too easily turned into something "manageable"—a "best practice" or, sadly, a "rule" to be followed.

When Ambrose was elected bishop of Milan in 374, Christianity was a tolerated religion but not yet the preferred religion of the state. His experience of many religions mirrors our own. In the swelter of many competing "spiritual paths," he recognized that the way in which one becomes Christian would reveal its distinctive faith and life. Using art, architecture, music, ritual, inscription, and preaching, he set forth a rich and striking way of life capable of responding to deep human need with the gospel of Jesus Christ. One image, one word alone would not do. Is it any different for us?

For reflection and discussion

1. What do you consider your primary understanding or image of Christian baptism? What, for you, happens to someone in baptism? Has your reading of this chapter expanded your appreciation of the richness of Christian baptism? If not, why not?

2. Can you remember a sermon or sermons which opened for you the meanings of baptism? If so, what do you remember and how did such preaching expand or challenge your experience and understanding of being a baptized Christian?

3. For close to two thousand years, Christians have been composing hymn texts and canticles which reflect the rich and diverse interpretations of baptism found in the New Testament. That is, Christians have been singing into their memories the many meanings of baptism. What one hymn or song text speaks significantly to you of your baptismal identity?

4. One claim made in this chapter is that diverse understandings of baptism respond to diverse needs among the members of the worshiping assembly. What might be one understanding of baptism that responds to a real need of yours?

5. From the font, one comes to the table. While we have been speaking of baptismal faith and life in this little book, it is important to remember that baptismal identity is always eucharistic identity. The Holy Communion or Holy Eucharist holds in continuing availability all that has happened in Holy Baptism. Is the connection between font and table—the first leading to the second—apparent in the preaching teaching, and practice of your congregation? If not, why not?

5
Immersed in the World

O God, kindle Thou in my heart within
A flame of love to my neighbor,
To my foe, to my friend, to my kindred all,
To the brave, to the knave, to the thrall,
O Son of the loveliest Mary,
From the lowliest thing that liveth,
To the Name that is highest of all.

The late medieval culture of the sixteenth-century reformers was focused spiritually on leaving this world. The influence of neoplatonic philosophy had become strong in Christian faith and life, and this philosophy suggested that one's purpose is to leave this world of fragility, diminishment, and death for a celestial realm in which the intangible soul might enjoy union with the immaterial divine. Indeed, the late medieval church suggested that baptism was the event at which one began this journey toward one's eternal reward—aided, of course, by the power of God's grace, the word and sacraments, and one's good works. Thus, baptism initiated one into the search for salvation, guided by God's grace and dependent upon human cooperation with that grace. It was a search marked by a powerful emotional sensibility—for who would want to be separated for all eternity from one's family, one's friends, the Savior, and the Creator of heaven and earth?

At the same time, the church had become a hierarchical structure which mirrored the social stratifications of the larger culture. While all were baptized into Christ, only those who entered vowed religious life or were ordained to public ministry could claim a "vocation" from the Spirit. Indeed, the late medieval search for salvation seemed to be a quest best achieved by leaving behind ordinary life in this world and entering the monastic cloister or becoming a celibate priest. In the stratification of holiness, those who had seemingly "left all" to follow Christ—those who were professionally engaged in religious leadership and life—could be seen as having a better chance of succeeding in that widespread search for God's grace and mercy.

What, then, of the ordinary, baptized Christian—the layperson who worked in the world, a place perceived by some church theologians as filled with many temptations to sin, a sphere of life somehow less "spiritual" than monastery or church? Well, one could work hard, spiritually, by receiving the Eucharist, confessing one's sins, completing one's penance, praying with greater diligence, going on a pilgrimage, offering whatever charity one could to the needy, requesting favors from the saints, or even buying a spiritual favor that might help one advance on the path to heaven. For the baptized layperson—prince or peasant, serving girl or duchess—such spiritual exercises could enlarge the grace received at baptism, strengthen one's faith, and expand one's charitable deeds—hoping that one had done enough or had sufficient faith or believed the "right" things to merit a gracious judgment on the Last Day. Hoping . . . but not sure.

Made right with God for life with others on earth

It was that lack of certainty which drove Martin Luther and other reformers to question the theology and practice of late-medieval

Christianity. It was his and their assiduous study of the New Testament which called into question the very idea that one could be made right with God, "justified," by virtue of what one does to gain favor in the sight of God. It was the simple declaration of Paul—"We hold that a person is justified by faith apart from works prescribed by the law" (Rom. 3:28)—that turned upside down the received tradition of the medieval theologians. It was this teaching—that God justifies persons by grace and grace alone—that called into question the social stratification of Christian life and the role of baptism in that life. In effect, Luther and his reforming colleagues in Germany, Switzerland, and England reversed the direction of the late-medieval search for God and conversely insisted that it is God who advances toward fragile, diminished, and dying humans in this world, an advent revealed with utter clarity in the birth, life, death, and resurrection of Jesus Christ, a movement that continues out into the world as the baptized serve their neighbors in need. By insisting first on God's saving advance toward humanity, rather than humanity's search for God, Luther and his colleagues placed the promise and reality of salvation, rather than the search for salvation, at the beginning of a Christian's life—at the font. In effect, they argued that a person does not begin the journey toward one's eternal reward at baptism. They claimed, rather, that the promise and gift of salvation are offered freely in baptism itself. Thus freed from the need and anxiety to find spiritual favor with God so that one might ultimately enjoy spiritual union with God, *the baptized person is free to live his or her life in this world as a Christian, as Christ, to and for the other.* Union with Christ—marriage to the beloved—takes place at the font; the rest of one's life is living into the deep meanings of that union. Rather than looking with trepidation toward the Last Judgment at life's end, Luther insisted that the Last Judgment has already taken place at the beginning of one's life, in the washing with water and the Word of God, in that washing which draws one into reign of God's grace and mercy. God's advance toward humanity in baptism thus issued forth in the Christian's advance into the world of daily life; a world, nonetheless, marked by incredible need. Quite simply, freed from the anxious search to find favor with God, baptized Christians could now to attend to life in this world, to care for real human needs, to listen for and discern and live out their distinctive vocations in ordinary times and ordinary places.

In 1520, Luther published a call for the reform of the church, a reform to be promoted not by bishops or priests but by *laypersons*: the baptized rulers of the German nation. Entitled "To the Christian Nobility of the German Nation Concerning the Reform of the Christian Estate," this urgent call for immediate change was rooted in the teaching on justification by grace, a teaching which was poured into the practice of baptism. While late-medieval Christians recognized that there was a "spiritual estate" made up of baptized bishops, priests, and members of religious orders and a "temporal estate" made up of baptized princes, artisans, and farmers, Luther viewed these two estates as artificial and unbiblical. "All Christians are truly of the spiritual estate, and there is no difference among them except that of office. . . . This is because we all have one baptism, one gospel, one faith, and are all Christian alike; for baptism makes us spiritual and a Christian people" (*LW* 44:127). What was Luther implying? Could it be that in the sacrament of baptism, one enters into an egalitarian community where cultural or religious social statuses (e.g., bishop or prince, farmer or monk) are dissolved? He continues: "We are all consecrated priests through baptism, as St. Peter says in 1 Peter 2 [:9], 'You are a royal priesthood and priestly realm'" (*LW* 44:127). In a culture where social and economic stratification seemed "normal," the suggestion that all Christians are fundamentally equal by virtue of baptism would have sounded revolutionary.

Consecrated with Christ as servants in the world

As members of the one "spiritual estate,"—the body of Christ—the work of each member is of considerable value. One could no longer claim that being a pastor or priest was somehow more valuable, or holier, or closer to God than being a teacher or a banker. "A cobbler, a smith, a peasant—each has the work and office of his trade, and yet they are all consecrated priests [in baptism]. Further, everyone must benefit and serve every other by means of his own work or office so that in this way many kinds of work may be done for the bodily and spiritual welfare of the community" (*LW* 44:128). And, thus, Luther redefined the term "vocation," rejecting the late-medieval notion that only the ordained or vowed monks and nuns have a "calling" from God. Instead, he insisted that every baptized Christian, filled with the power and presence of the Holy Spirit, is called to recognize that his or her work in the world is the very means through which one's faith becomes active in love for the neighbor in need. Rather than initiating one into a lifelong search for salvation or bringing a person into a private relationship with God, baptism consecrates the adult or the infant to a life of faith made active in public service, in service to the common good. Such public service can be recognized in what God provides all creation: night for rest and day for labor; water, fire, soil, and air—the earthy things which provide food and drink; the human community. All these gifts are offered to creatures before they even ask and through all these gifts all creatures are sustained in life. Thus, Luther—with his vivid sacramental imagination—affirmed the incarnational principle at the heart of Christianity: just as the hidden and unseen God provides sustenance for all living things through the ordinary, mundane, and earthy gifts of creation, so too the hidden God is clothed in human form: the Word becomes flesh in Jesus of Nazareth (John 1:14). And, this, too: the invisible God continues to be "clothed" in those washed in the waters of baptism:

> What else is all our work to God—whether in the fields, in the garden, in the city, in the house, in war, or in government—but . . . a child's performance, by which he wants to give his gifts in the fields, at home, and everywhere else? These are the *masks of God* behind which he wants to remain concealed and

> do all things . . . [God] could give children without using men
> and women but does not want to do this. Instead, he joins
> man and woman so that it appears to be the work of man
> and woman, and yet he does it under the cover of such masks
> (*LW* 14:114).

Such a claim—the regular work of baptized Christians in the world is a veritable "mask" through which God continues to create, save, and sustain earth and its creatures—rejected the notion that the Christian way is a way to leave this world or a way to be caught up in a "private" relationship with God, cut off from the economic, social, and political dimensions of life. The reformers insisted that baptism leads Christians into life on this earth, to enter and engage this world as public agents of the reign of God revealed in Jesus Christ. Rejecting the neoplatonic and Gnostic tendencies within the Christian tradition, the reformers urged the Christian people to let their faith, their trust in God, become active publicly in many initiatives which served the common good, initiatives which were rooted in the witness of the New Testament. This invitation was in contrast to the practice of medieval Christianity in which social welfare was sponsored by cathedral clergy or members of religious orders. The reformers asked *the entire baptized assembly* to bear responsibility for each other and for their brothers and sisters in need.

Such an invitation reshaped and continues to challenge perceptions of ordinary work and daily life. While it might have been and remains easy to imagine that religious leaders, lay and ordained, do "spiritual" work while everyone else participates in "secular" work, the reformers' insistence that baptism "consecrates" all women, men, and children as "priests" who "minister" in the world offers a robust reassessment of seemingly "worldly work." If there is truth in the claim that a Christian's profession—as a businessperson, educator, political official, healthcare provider, news investigator, repair person, homemaker, or whatever it may be—is a "mask" of God, would not one have to ask how one's daily labor is a natural sacrament of God's creating, saving, and sustaining presence in the world? Would not such a vision of one's presence in daily life challenge one to consider how one's life and work participates in the advance of God's gracious and merciful presence in the world—not stopping at the font or at the church door—but into the very places where Jesus himself was to be found? After all, he spent little time in the holy precincts of the Temple but was found in village and town—in daily life—interacting with ordinary people who needed companionship and nourishment, forgiveness and enlightenment, healing and liberation. "One could very well say that the course of the world, and especially the doing of the saints, are God's mask, under which God conceals himself and so marvelously exercises dominion" (*LW* 45:331). As a baptized Christian, I am called to serve as a "mask" of God's presence in daily life; does such a claim cause one to pause and ponder?

A charter for baptismal living

Tucked away in the pages of contemporary worship books and hymnals is a series of questions directed toward those who desire to reaffirm the baptismal covenant. Please note: their very simplicity can lead some people to overlook them. Their unassuming nature might encourage some people to rush through them, giving them little thought. But the questions merit our attention. They suggest that faith is not simply the intellectual affirmation of a series of propositions about God but a way of living in the world as one who has been washed, marked, clothed, and communed in Christ. They suggest that baptism initiates one into a way of living in the world, of making commitments to others. They set forth the shape of baptismal living. The presider asks those who are making public affirmation of baptism:

> Do you intend to continue in the covenant God made with you
> in holy baptism:
> to live among God's faithful people,
> to hear the word of God and share in the Lord's supper,
> to proclaim the good news of God in Christ through word
> and deed,
> to serve all people, following the example of Jesus,
> and to strive for justice and peace in all the earth?
> (*Evangelical Lutheran Worship*, pp. 236, 237;
> *Book of Common Prayer*, pp. 304–305)

A seeking soul may ask, "What does it mean to be baptized?" For the person who has no idea what to say or the one who has far too much to say, these five questions might be a good place to begin. Consider, for instance, the words of the German martyr Dietrich Bonhoeffer: "Christianity means community through Jesus Christ and in Jesus Christ. No Christian community is more or less than this . . . We belong to one another only through and in Jesus Christ." He continues, "What does this mean? It means that a Christian needs others because of Jesus Christ" (*Life Together*, p. 21). In a culture which prizes the individual and rewards individual success, Christian baptism highlights, deepens, and expands the truth of who we actually are: *social beings created by God for life with each other*. In contrast to the cultural illusion of the "self-made" person whose greatest "bliss" is to follow his or her own path, baptism reveals this singular truth: humans are interdependent creatures, from birth to death. No one, not one single person, is ever "self-made." Baptism initiates one into the shared life of God's faithful people, into a body of companions. As with the ancient Hebrews and with Jesus and his disciples, we journey through life together—fully aware that we will experience bickering and assistance, common cause and misunderstanding, sad divisions and the bonds of affection. For the church is nothing less than the very human body of the risen Christ—a great and diverse tribe of water-washed, stumbling, Spirit-strengthened, failing, forgiven, at times small-minded, at times prophetic, nourished, and—hopefully—nourishing people. "I am the vine," says the beloved, "you are the branches. Those who abide in me and I in them bear much fruit, because apart from me you can do nothing" (John 15:5).

While many churches list an array of different groups one can join for study, service, or fellowship, and while these groups may play a significant role in bonding participants, they are like planets floating around a radiant center: the assembly of the baptized gathered on Sunday, the day of resurrection, for the proclamation and homiletical interpretation of its holy book and the celebration of Christ's holy supper. At the heart of Christian life is *the communal encounter with the risen Christ who nourishes his living body from the table of the word and the table of the supper*. While worship leaders and assembly do indeed prepare for and celebrate the liturgy, the seeking soul and the long-timer are both called to remember that the baptized gather—as the body of Christ—in the presence of the Creator of heaven and earth, in the presence of the wounded and risen Lord Jesus, in the presence and power of the life-giving Spirit who draws the many into one body, one voice. While musicians support song, lectors read from the lectionary, and ministers distribute bread and wine, all these very ordinary actions point to and serve this simple but oft-forgotten truth: the baptized gather in the presence of God—that holy mystery greater than our words and images and actions. The baptized, catechumens, and visitors stand, sit, kneel, sing, speak, and move in the presence of the holy mystery that has brought the universe and every seeking soul into existence, the mystery of the creating Word becoming flesh, the mystery of the rushing and uncontrollable Spirit who enlivens what may appear to be dormant or dying. The American writer, Annie Dillard, points to this mystery at the heart of Christian worship:

On the whole, I do not find Christians . . . sufficiently sensible of conditions. Does anyone have the foggiest idea what sort of power we so blithely invoke? Or, as I suspect, does no one believe a word of it? The church is children playing on the floor with their chemistry sets, mixing up a batch of TNT to kill a Sunday morning . . . We should all be wearing crash helmets . . . ushers should lash us to our pews. For the sleeping god may awake someday and take offense, or the waking god may draw us out to where we can never return (*Teaching a Stone to Talk*, p. 52–53).

Perhaps worship in word and sacrament has become so user-friendly, so chatty and so chummy, so "relevant," so easily divided along culturally formed musical tastes, that far too many have forgotten the truth that we welcome the newly baptized into the presence of that "splendor burning at the heart of all things: the flame of living love which lights the law of mystic death that works the mystic birth" (Evelyn Underhill, "Corpus Christi"). What does it mean to be baptized? It may, indeed, mean many things but it certainly means this: gathering with the local assembly around the "splendor burning at the heart of all things" revealed in word spoken, sung, and prayed, in a saving life broken as bread and poured out as wine for the life of the world, "a flame of living love" that may draw us out to where we never expected we would go.

The assumption alive in many forms of American Christianity is that a series of propositions or theological ideas alone constitute the life of faith. For instance, one might assume that personal or communal assent to the idea of the Holy Trinity or justification by grace or an inclusive church or bread received as Body is at the heart of baptismal living. But if one carefully considers the theological claims just mentioned, it becomes apparent that all of them are ways of shaping daily living from the perspective of font and altar. Christians confess their faith in the Triune God—Father, Son, and Spirit—not as a neat though abstract description of God but as an affirmation of the Holy Three who encircle each Christian with creative, saving, and enlightening powers. The seeking soul asks, "What does it mean to be baptized?" It may well mean this: that *the baptized and communed Christian allows this creative, saving, and enlightening presence to shape his or her words and deeds in daily life.* After all, think of the alternative! Does one want to live as a person committed to diminishment, oppression, and ignorance in a world that already experiences too much of these dehumanizing powers?

Christians claim the gracious and justifying action of God so that they might be known as gracious persons rather than aloof or merciless persons. Christians welcome anyone, regardless of gender, orientation, race, ethnicity, and socioeconomic status, through the inclusive waters of baptism into the reign of God and the church that serves that reign in human life. Christians continue this inclusive baptismal practice so that they become a people who first recognize each other and other persons as those created by a loving God and redeemed by the blood of the Lamb—not as "categories" in a demographic grid. We give thanks and ask that bread and wine, ordinary gifts of earth and human labor, might be for us the body and blood of our Lord Jesus Christ so that we might be more clearly and more faithfully a people who nourish others in word and deed. This is to say that what we have received among God's faithful people in word and sacrament is intended to shape our daily lives. Christians gather in the presence of the "splendor burning at the heart of all things" so that this burning, loving, forgiving, challenging, nourishing, and healing presence might shape our words and deeds in daily life. The long-ago baptized and the newly baptized gather in the liturgy so that they, so that we, might continue the liturgy in the daily life. What does it mean to be baptized?

The Christian assembly welcomes people, proclaims the grace of God, receives forgiveness, celebrates rites of healing, gives thanks at table, shares the holy nourishment of bread and wine so that the people of God might be a welcoming, gracious, forgiving and reconciling, healing, thankful, and nourishing presence in daily life. Really, this is not rocket science, yet it remains puzzling why so many teachers and preachers find it difficult to recognize the intimate relationship between sound liturgy and daily life. Christians celebrate this ensemble of actions we call rituals or liturgies because they are rooted in the memory and presence of the risen Christ who welcomed people into companionship, who proclaimed the grace and mercy of the reign of God, who offered forgiveness and reconciliation, who healed freely those who were isolated by trouble of mind or body, who provided food and drink and gave himself away in love as body broken, as blood spilled. Christians do these things together so that they, so that we, might *serve all people, following the example of Jesus.* Interesting word there: *all* people. Not just those people who are like us, who appear regularly on our dinner invitation list. Not just those people who mirror one's racial, educational, and socioeconomic status. Not just those people who share one's religious identity. Troubling word there: *all* people. "O God, we give you thanks that you have set before us this feast, the body and blood of your Son. By your Spirit strengthen us to serve all in need and to give ourselves away as bread for the hungry, through Jesus Christ our Lord" (*Evangelical Lutheran Worship*, p. 114). The seeking and curious soul wonders: is it a challenge to say Amen to the prayer and thus assent to its implication for one's daily life?

New Testament scholars point out that St. Paul begins and frequently peppers his letters with these words, "grace and peace to you." Grace and peace. Given that he lived in one of the most violent empires in human history, one might have expected a Roman citizen, which he was, to begin a letter with words that aptly described every day human experience, what just about everyone thought was normal in daily life: Harshness. Brutality. Impoverishment. Injustice. Conquest. Defeat. Slavery. As the English poet W.H. Auden once wrote: "the slogan of hell is, Eat or be eaten." How odd, then, his greeting must have sounded for a people swimming in a world of violence. "Grace to you and peace from God our Father and the Lord Jesus Christ" (Rom. 1:7). Was this simply a polite greeting for his fellow Christians, something one might expect from a "religious" or "spiritual" person? Or was he suggesting something else, something, perhaps, far more revolutionary than a sweet, pious greeting? Could it be that St. Paul filled his every letter with greetings and farewells—marked by grace and peace—because he recognized in the Lord Jesus an alternative to the harshness and brutality of the world in which they lived? Could it be that he was clearly claiming that those who were and are baptized into the life of Christ, are "clothed" in Christ, are clothed in his commitment to live as a person of peace in striking counterpoint to a culture sated with the desire for military conquest and economic expansion by violent means? And would not living a life marked by grace and peace, by peacemaking, actually become noticeable in a culture where crucifixion was the preferred method to silence the voice, the way of life, rooted in the worship of the God of peace? "Now may the God of peace, who brought back from the dead our Lord Jesus, the great shepherd of the sheep . . . make you complete in everything good" (Heb. 13:20-21). Consider that blessing: the God of peace, who raised Jesus from a violent and public death crafted by the Roman army. Is it possible that baptismal living is *a living committed to the promotion of peace*, in a world culture that too frequently sanctions violence and violent methods? Is it possible, then, that the One who gives himself as broken body and shed blood desires to nourish the newly baptized and long-ago baptized in the peace of God, "which surpasses all understanding" (Phil. 4:7)?

One simple question: "Do you intend to continue in the covenant God made with you in holy baptism"? Yet, this simple question moves us from the intimacy of God's faithful people gathered around word and sacrament and into a world which cries out for nourishment and reconciliation, healing and peace. Not one without the other: both the support of God's faithful people and the challenge to serve all in need; both word and sacrament and the pursuit of peace. Not one without the other.

For reflection and discussion

1. While there is a profound personal dimension to Christian baptism—it is you and you alone who are washed in the name of the Holy Three and the waters of the font—there is also a profound social or public dimension to Christian baptism. One is marked as a public figure, a public representative of the gospel of Jesus Christ. If this is a new awareness for you, how are you dealing with it?

2. While many Christian congregations are happy to speak much about baptismal vocation in the world, what are the concrete ways in which members of your congregation are invited to embody, to live out that vocation in daily life? Do sermons, classes, workshops, or retreats invite a serious discussion of the challenges to live out one's baptismal and eucharistic identity on a daily basis?

3. In this chapter, we have spent some time focusing on the questions asked of those who will affirm their baptism. What is your response to the notion that these questions can serve as a charter for baptismal and eucharistic living in the world: too ambiguous or just right or never thought of them before?

4. Historians and sociologists of early Christianity claim that people were attracted to the emerging, minority Christian movement because its members displayed a distinctive *way of living* in the world. People noticed them. Such notice got them in trouble when they objected to certain cultural values and practices. And such notice proved highly attractive to some people—though not all—in the cultures of the ancient Mediterranean. What would you say is distinctive and appealing about your congregation's way of living into its baptismal identity? Who would *not* be attracted to your way of life and why would you wish them well?

5. While many Christians pass or exchange "the peace" in the liturgy as a way of greeting other people in the worshiping assembly, the original intention of the gesture was to acknowledge that this community is committed to peace and reconciliation in the world, in

the region, in the town or city. By exchanging the peace, a person is actually committing himself or herself to work for peace in church and society. Is this your intention in greeting others with the peace of the risen Christ? If so, how are you or your congregation engaged in promoting peace and reconciliation publicly in your community or region?

6
An Invitation
and a Challenge

I heard the voice of Jesus say,
"Behold, I freely give
the living water, thirsty one;
stoop down and drink and live."

God's own flowing gracious life

If there is any image that captured the imagination of the women and men who were caught up in that tumultuous and complex phenomenon called the "Reformation" in the sixteenth century, it was the image of a stream or spring of fresh, flowing water. While many reformers would speak of "light breaking into a time of darkness," they constantly returned to the image of a spring or fountain of freely rushing water: "Follow the brook which flows from Christ and leads to the spring" (*LW* 24:70-71). Convinced that the life-giving waters of the gospel of Jesus Christ had been blocked up and overgrown with five hundred years of muddied teaching and practice, the reformers were intent on removing the blockage and letting the "pure" spring flow widely and deeply into Christian faith and life.

It should come as no surprise, then, that the reformers restored that ensemble of words and actions called baptism to a central place in the Christian imagination. The saving waters of the gospel of Jesus Christ were to flow into the human life through the word and the waters of the font. Indeed, their careful study of the New Testament uncovered not one but many interpretations of this primordial sacrament. Baptism is regeneration, being reborn in and through the Spirit (Titus 3:5-6; cf. John 3:1-10). It is being immersed in the death of Jesus—in the cross—and raised with him into a new way of living in the world (Rom. 6:1-11; cf. Mark 10:35-40). Baptism is being wed to Christ in an intimate and holy union (Eph. 5:26) and transferred, adopted, into the reign of the beloved son (Col. 1:12-14). Thus, Christian baptism calls upon and transfigures the experiences of birth from the womb, marriage to another, and burial at death as lively metaphors of its promise in human life.

Baptism bestows the forgiveness of sins and initiates one into the assembly that "devoted themselves to the apostles' teaching and fellowship, to the breaking of bread and the prayers" (Acts 2:42). Baptism consecrates infant and adult as members of a holy and priestly people who offer their lives in service to others in the world (1 Peter 2:4-10). In baptism, one is clothed in Christ—with women, men, and children, with Jews and Greeks, with poor and rich (Gal. 3:26-29), with persons of ambiguous sexuality (Acts 8:26-40). Through baptism, one is enlightened by the Spirit (Heb. 6:1-8; cf. John 4:1-42) and washed into "that great multitude," robed in white, singing before the throne of God and the Lamb, where hunger, thirst, and sorrow no longer rule (Rev. 7:9-17; cf. *Holy People*, p. 178). Thus, Christian baptism leads one into the energy field of grace and hope, orients one to another way of living in the world, initiates one into a great company of the most unlikely companions, and welcomes one to the supper of the

Lamb, the breaking of the bread, the heavenly banquet, and the great thanksgiving meal.

Before one can request it and after one asks for it, Christian baptism is the unmerited and gracious action of God. With the flowing and raining waters of the earth, baptism is offered to all; it falls and flows without discrimination and begins the dissolution of all that is not of Christ—a dying to the self as the center of one's imagination and a rebirth in grace to life with the Holy Three and one's neighbor—human and other-than-human. And this as well: all that baptism effects and promises is held in continuing availability in the Holy Eucharist, the Holy Communion. As many early Christian bishops preached: those who are born in the womb of the font are immediately brought to the breast of the Lord's altar, there to be nourished with food and drink. And all this without price, without demand, without coercion. All freely and openly given. Consequently, the preparation that leads to the font and the ongoing formation that flows from the waters are themselves the gracious actions of God mediated through companions, catechists, ministers, and the assembly in conversation, questions, worship and prayer, reflection on Scripture, service to others, discernment, and discovering and embracing one's calling in life.

A radical welcome surprising even Christians

Yet a culturally formed imagination might construe Christian baptism as just one more "rite of passage" or requirement for membership. Or, as one finds among some Christians, baptism is understood as the gate-keeper to an exclusive inner group of the "saved." Such was the perspective of Mrs. Ruby Turpin, one of the central figures in Flannery O'Connor's short story, "Revelation." A baptized Christian of the Deep South, Mrs. Turpin is a bigot who holds condescending pity for blacks and an almost heartless scorn for lower-class whites. She is baptized yet bigoted; a child of God yet one who holds a strong sense of her superiority over almost all other people. Indeed, she is genuinely grateful to

God when she considers all that she has and what she believes is her good disposition. There are moments, when encountering the poverty and apparent ugliness, laziness, and "unrighteousness" of others, that she can hardly keep from shouting out loud, "Thank you, Jesus!" so pleased is she with her good, Christian life—or say it this way: a life lived in withering judgment over others.

That is, until the moment when a young woman named Mary Grace, a physically unpleasant person in the eyes of Mrs. Turpin, tells this smug and rather plump "pillar" of church and community that she is nothing more than a warthog from hell. No compliment there and an incredible affront to Ruby Turpin. Stunned and so deeply offended by this bitter and angry outburst, she begins to wonder if the young girl's insult is a message from God. And once she entertains the notion that *God* could be speaking to her through this ugly and impertinent girl, she begins to ask angry questions of God. So fiercely does her anger arise, so thoroughly does it consume her that, once home and standing beside her pig pen, the evening sky dissolves into a vision—a vision of a long, swinging bridge reaching upward into heaven, yet a bridge which passes through a field filled with fire. Walking on that upward bound bridge she could see a vast tribe of people, among them "freaks" and "lunatics" shouting and clapping their way into heaven. She could see white-robed blacks and the "white trash scum" she so clearly disdained making their way heavenward. And last—last—in that endless procession, she recognized people just like herself: people who had always had a little of everything, upstanding people, good, white Christian people who had the God-given smarts to use well what God had given them. There they were, at the end of the line; not at the front where they should have been leading the poor, the riffraff, the "freaks." And as she viewed those who were walking at the end, seemingly good people, her own kith and kin, she was startled to see the expressions on their shocked and transfigured faces for "even their virtues were being burned away" ("Revelation," p. 508).

Before one can request it and after one asks for it, Christian baptism is the unmerited and gracious action of God. Set next to that ancient Christian claim is this: those who are perceived by society as "unclean," "undesirable," or "unrighteous," as "freaks," "trash," or "riffraff" are welcomed into Christ, wed to Christ, transferred into the reign of the beloved son, initiated into the company of holy priests, marked as Christ's own forever, enlightened by the Spirit, and washed into "that great multitude" that no one can count, robed in white, and singing before the throne of God and the Lamb. Here is the challenging question: Who would seek such a community in which "freaks" and "lunatics" eat from the same loaf of bread and drink from the same cup as "good" and "upstanding" people? Paul writes that baptism is not for the few but for the many, for all people: women and men, Gentile and Jew, slave and free (Gal. 3:26-29). It is the *rejection* or exclusion of those who are personally or socially perceived as "outsiders" or "undesirables" that now is strikingly *rejected* in the practice of Christian baptism. Persons are not excluded in baptism but rather *the temptation—among individuals and societies—to exclude some people, indeed whole groups of people* who appear to be insufficiently "worthy" to enter the community of faith.

One recognizes the inability of some to accept others at baptism in the 1989 film, *Romero*, a biography of Oscar Romero, the martyred archbishop of San Salvador (+1980). A young mother, from one of the wealthiest and most powerful families in the nation, comes to the archbishop after a Sunday mass and asks when he will be able to baptize her newborn daughter. He tells her that she and her family can come to the cathedral on a Sunday afternoon when baptisms are normally scheduled. "Do you mean a *public* baptism?" she asks with incredulity. "We expected you and you alone to baptize our baby in private." Again, he invites her to the Sunday afternoon baptism. "But isn't that the time when all those poor Indians bring their children for baptism? I couldn't possibly have my child baptized in the same water with them." Stunned by his insistence that she and her privileged family will receive no special treatment, she walks away, angry and confused.

And so one wonders: did she actually discern the radical inclusion of baptism and elect to forego it?

As Ambrose notes, the cross of Jesus Christ has been thrown into the font of baptism. That is, the mercy of God, revealed in the crucified Christ, transfigures the meaning of Christian baptism: it is neither a requirement for membership nor the gate-keeper to an exclusive group of the "saved." Rather, a challenging gift of grace, an uncommon birth into a community where an alternative vision of "life together" is attempted, practiced, and, if truth be told, at times abandoned. Such abandonment was diagnosed by the Lutheran pastor and German martyr, Dietrich Bonhoeffer. Living in a country that was called the "cradle of the Reformation," a country in which the vast majority of the population identified themselves as Lutheran ("evangelical") or Roman Catholic Christians, Bonhoeffer came to the striking conclusion that the preaching and practice of "cheap grace" had "Christianized" the nation but done nothing to transform the lives of its people. While Germans believed that their baptism offered a promise which would be fulfilled at the end of their lives—the promise of eternal life—they seemed incapable, in Bonhoeffer's eyes, of recognizing the challenge, the warning, that accompanies baptism: this gracious action initiates one into a radically different way of seeing and living now, with others, on this earth. The preaching and practice of a *culturally conformed gospel* simply yet tragically leaves Christians with the patina of Christian religiosity:

> If grace is the data for my Christian life, it means that I set out to live the Christian life in the world with all my sins justified beforehand. I can go and sin as much as I like and rely on this grace to forgive me, for after all the world is justified in principle by grace. I can therefore cling to my bourgeois (middle-class) secular existence, and remain as I was before, but with the added

assurance that the grace of God will cover me. It is under the influence of this kind of "grace" that the world has been made "Christian," but at the cost of secularizing the Christian religion as never before (*Cost of Discipleship*, p. 54).

For Bonhoeffer, Christian baptism makes one a disciple of Jesus Christ. Who would argue with this claim? But the *implication* of the claim is quite significant: there could be no other competing loyalty that trumps one's fundamental identity as a Christian; no other person or nation, idea or practice in which the Christian places his or her ultimate trust; no conforming of the gospel of Jesus Christ into a palatable dish easily consumed by one's current culture. Christian baptism could not be one more identity marker, one more layer of clothing added to one's political, ethnic, economic, and educational wardrobe. It could not be about leaving "secular" life for an hour or so on Sunday—to be reminded that one's sins are forgiven or that one is loved by God—and then returning to one's ordinary life relatively unchanged. For Bonhoeffer, the preaching and teaching of "cheap grace" is the proclamation of beloved words—"grace," "forgiveness," "mercy," "inclusion"—without the following of Jesus Christ and without the enactment of those words in daily life. His warning, first spoken in Nazi Germany, strikes at the heart of contemporary "user-friendly" American congregations:

> The price that we are having to pay today in the shape of the collapse of the organized Church is only the inevitable consequence of our policy of making grace available to all at too low a cost. We gave away the word and sacraments wholesale, we baptized, confirmed, and absolved a whole nation unasked and without condition. Our humanitarian sentiment made us give that which was holy to the scornful and unbelieving. We poured forth unending streams of grace. But the call to follow Jesus in the narrow way was hardly ever heard. Where were those truths

which impelled the early Church to institute the catechumenate, which enabled a strict watch to be kept over the frontier between the church and the world, and afforded adequate protection for costly grace? What had happened to all those warnings of Luther's against preaching the gospel in such a manner as to make men [sic] rest secure in their ungodly living? (*The Cost of Discipleship*, p. 58)

Bonhoeffer recognized how easy it was for his fellow Christians—baptized, confirmed, and communed—to support a political regime intent on doing violence to its own people. The practice and theology of Christian baptism had been narrowed to the promise of eternal life or one's entrance into the German Christian nation. It thus became impossible for most Christians to recognize how they were being seduced by a vision of "life together," which relied—relied—upon gender, ethnic, racial, political and socioeconomic divisions and animosity to succeed. Such a weak and culturally conformed view of baptism prevented Christians from recognizing the public character of Christian life. "When he called men [sic] to follow him, Jesus was summoning them to a visible act of obedience. To follow Jesus was a public act. Baptism is a public event, for it is the means whereby a member is grafted on to the visible body of Christ. The breach with the world, which has been effected in Christ, can no longer remain hidden. It must come out into the open" (*The Cost of Discipleship*, p. 259).

And what was the implication of living baptism publicly, of following Christ rather than a government legally elected by the people, of being marginalized by "good" and "upstanding" Christians? Perhaps you know the end of the story. Pastor Bonhoeffer was executed at a prison camp on April 9, 1945, for his resistance to the Nazi regime. Could one then say that he was executed because he was faithful to the baptismal covenant in all its grace as well as in its warning that one's life in this world will be forever changed?

Two words are always needed

The fundamentalist temptation will always knock at the door of the Christian imagination and ask for a hearing. The fundamentalist voice will claim that there is only one way to understand God, the Bible, the saving work of Christ, and the life of a Christian. In a world marked by religious and cultural pluralism, economic fragility, military conflicts, and environmental degradation, it is not difficult to see how one could find much consolation in such a monochromatic and unequivocal view of Christian faith and life. Yet it will not do for those who actually read the Bible's many voices, consider the diverse ways in which salvation can be experienced, and recognize that the Spirit, wild and lively, will animate more ways of being Christian than all the theologians could ever imagine.

In this other way of being Christian, it will always take more than one word, one image, one idea, or one practice to imagine the rich and fertile dimensions of Christian existence. One word will not do. We always need more, at least two if not three or four or five. Thus, baptism as gracious and unmerited gift needs to be placed next to baptism as warning or challenge that one's view of and living in this world will be forever changed. Or this: baptismal preparation needs to be placed next to baptismal liturgy which needs to be placed next to lifelong baptismal and eucharistic formation. Or this: public baptism leads to a public life. Or this: "my" baptism weds me to Christ and all those whom Christ loves and they to me and, thus, no longer "mine" but "ours."

Or this: baptism forgives sin but also welcomes into the life of the Holy Trinity, gives and nourishes faith, joins one to unlikely companions, opens up a closed sense of time, binds one to a global community, bestows one's eternal dignity and destiny in Christ, plants one in a communion of ancestors who are still conversing with us through art, writing, song, architecture, and ritual. Or this: the font welcomes the waters of the earth, God's own precious creation yet increasingly fouled by our collective sin. Or this: one is always failing and always forgiven. Or this: water washing and the binding of the Three Names and fragrant oil and white clothing and burning flame and thunderous welcome and walking to the altar and eating from the one loaf and drinking from the one cup and walking out the door, marked as Christ's own forever, walking steadfastly into a world marked by incredible need.

One word, one image will not account for the inexhaustible riches we enter in Christian baptism. There will always be more. There is the gift. And there is the challenge.

Acknowledgments

Quotations at the beginning of each chapter are in the public domain.

Introduction
"Here the innocent sheep"
Baptismal inscription at the Basilica of St. Peter in Rome

Chapter 1
"Here springs the fountain of life"
Baptismal inscription at St. John Lateran in Rome

Chapter 2
"Christians live in their own countries"
Epistle of Mathetes to Diognetus 5

Chapter 3
"Anyone who comes to me"
John 6:37

Chapter 4
"Fountain of grace, rich, full, and free"
James Edmeston

Chapter 5
"O God, kindle Thou in my heart within"
Celtic invocation

Chapter 6
"I heard the voice of Jesus say"
Horatius Bonar

Bibliography

Foundational Texts

A Baptism Sourcebook
Edited by Robert Baker, Larry Nyberg, and Victoria Tufano
Chicago: Liturgy Training Publications, 1993.

The Book of Common Prayer
According to the Use of the Episcopal Church
New York: The Church Hymnal Corporation, 1979.

Deiss, Lucien
Springtime of the Liturgy
Collegeville, Minn.: Liturgical Press, 1979.

Evangelical Lutheran Worship
Evangelical Lutheran Church in America
Minneapolis: Augsburg Fortress, 2006.

Luther, Martin
Luther's Works [American Edition]
St. Louis: Concordia Publishing House and Philadelphia: Fortress
Press, 1958-1967.

Saint Ambrose: Theological and Dogmatic Works
Vol. 44 in The Fathers of the Church, translated by Roy Deferrari
Washington, D.C.: The Catholic University of America Press, 1963.

1. The Baptism of Jesus in River and Cross

Crossan, John Dominic
Jesus: A Revolutionary Biography
San Francisco: Harper Collins, 1994.

Kavanagh, Aidan
The Shape of Christian Baptism: The Rite of Christian Initiation
Collegeville, Minn.: Liturgical Press, 1991.

Lathrop, Gordon
Holy People: A Liturgical Ecclesiology
Minneapolis: Fortress Press, 1999.

Romero, Oscar
A Martyr's Message of Hope: Six Homilies
Kansas City: Celebration Books, 1981.

2. The Catechism of Culture

Farley, Edward
Deep Symbols: Their Postmodern Effacement and Reclamation
Valley Forge, Penn.: Trinity International, 1996.

Gallagher, Michael
Clashing Symbols: An Introduction to Faith and Culture
Mahwah, N.J.: Paulist Press, 2004.

Kavanaugh, John
*Following Christ in a Consumer Culture: The Spirituality
of Cultural Resistance*
Maryknoll, N.Y.: Orbis Books, 1981, 1991, 2006.

Tillich, Paul
Theology of Culture
Edited by Robert Kimball
New York: Oxford University Press, 1959.

3. Entering and Leaving the Water

Johnson, Maxwell
The Rites of Initiation: Their Evolution and Interpretation
Collegeville, Minn.: Liturgical Press, 2007.

McElligott, Anne
The Catechumenal Process
New York: Church Publishing, 1990.

Weil, Louis
Theology of Worship
Cambridge, Mass.: Cowley Publications, 2001.

*Welcome to Christ: A Lutheran Introduction to
the Catechumenate*
Edited by Samuel Torvend
Minneapolis: Augsburg Fortress, 1997.

4. The Many Meanings of Christian Baptism

Ferguson, Everett
*Baptism in the Early Church: History, Theology, and Liturgy
in the First Five Centuries*
Grand Rapids, Mich.: Eerdmans, 2009.

Johnson, Maxwell
Images of Baptism
Chicago: Liturgy Training Publications, 2001.

Ramshaw, Gail
Words around the Font
Chicago: Liturgy Training Publications, 2004.

Stauffer, S. Anita
On Baptismal Fonts: Ancient and Modern
London: Grove Press, 1994.

Yarnold, Edward
The Awe-Inspiring Rites of Initiation
Collegeville, Minn.: Liturgical Press, 1994.

5. Immersed in the World

Bushkofsky, Dennis and Craig Satterlee
Using Evangelical Lutheran Worship: The Christian Life, Baptism, and Life Passages
Minneapolis: Augsburg Fortress, 2008.

Dillard, Annie
Teaching a Stone to Talk: Expeditions and Encounters
New York: Harper Collins, 1982.

Inside Out: Worship in an Age of Mission
Edited by Thomas Schattauer
Minneapolis: Fortress Press, 1999.

Lathrop, Gordon
Holy Ground: A Liturgical Cosmology
Minneapolis: Fortress Press, 2003.

McLaughlin, Nancy Ann
Do You Believe? Living the Baptismal Covenant
New York: Morehouse, 2006.

6. An Invitation and a Challenge

Bonhoeffer, Dietrich
The Cost of Discipleship
Translated by R. H. Fuller
New York: Macmillan, 1963.
O'Connor, Flannery
The Complete Stories
New York: Farrar, Straus, and Giroux, 1971.

Young, John Sacret
Romero
Directed by John Duigan
Pacific Palisades, Calif.: Paulist Productions, 1989.